STRANGER THAN FICTION

I have repeatedly been asked to write my life story. After all, it has been a full, exciting life and I have had two marriages; three daughters; and up to date, thirteen grandchildren and three great grandchildren and written nearly two hundred novels.

Many of my relatives and friends seem to think that it would be a pity if I didn't put on record a few of the strange things that have happened in my life. I shall tell the truth, 'the whole truth and nothing but the truth!'

BY AN OLD 'FIDELIS' GIRL.

**Also by the same author,
and available in Coronet Books:**

Cyprus Love Affair
Forbidden
House of The Seventh Cross
Gay Defeat
Do Not Go My Love
I Should Have Known
The Unlit Fire
Shatter The Sky
The Strong Heart
The Secret Hour
Nightingale's Song
It Wasn't Love
Fever Of Love
Climb To The Stars
Slave Woman
Second Best
Lightning Strikes Twice
Loving And Giving
Moment Of Love
Restless Heart
The Untrodden Snow
Betrayal
Twice Have I Loved
The Noble One
The Snow Must Return
Never Give All
Brief Ecstasy
Desire Is Blind
Never Look Back
Infatuation
You Have Chosen
Strange Meeting
Dark Corridor
To Love Again

Stranger than Fiction

Denise Robins
Her Life Story

CORONET BOOKS
Hodder and Stoughton

Copyright © 1965 by Denise Robins

First published in Great Britain 1965 by
Hodder and Stoughton Limited

Coronet Edition 1974
Second impression 1977

Printed in Great Britain for
Hodder and Stoughton Paperbacks,
a division of Hodder and Stoughton Ltd.,
Mill Road, Dunton Green, Sevenoaks, Kent
(Editorial Office : 47 Bedford Square,
London, WC1 3DP)
by Richard Clay (The Chaucer Press), Ltd.,
Bungay, Suffolk

ISBN 0 340 18877 4

FOR MY FAMILY

Fiction is Truth's elder sister.
Obviously. No one in the world knew what
truth was till someone had told a story.

From an Address: Royal Literary Society,
June, 1926.

ILLUSTRATIONS

Between pages 96 and 97

1 (*a*) D.R., aged 4, with mother
　(*b*) D.R. at 11
　(*c*) D.R., aged 19, as V.A.D. in First World War
2 (*a*) Neill, 1939. Armband initials stand for Instructor Fire Control
　(*b*) Our Wedding Day—30th October, 1939
3 (*a*) Roland Pertwee—author, and my greatest friend
　(*b*) Michael, his son, who has written the foreword to this book
4 (*a*) The Sutton family (daughter Eve). From left to right: Murray, Rosalind and her husband Milan, and Annabel
　(*b*) The Chadwick family (daughter Anne). From left to right: Pippa, Pauline-Belinda, myself, and Anne
5 　The Clark family (daughter Pat)
　(*a*) Pat with grandson Graeme
　(*b*) Iain Campbell Clark (Pat's son)
　(*c*) Nicola (Pat's daughter)
6 (*a*) Annabel Sutton, my grand-daughter
　(*b*) My eldest daughter, Eve
7 (*a*) R.N.A. Dinner 1963, Barbara Cartland at 'mike'. 'The President' between Ian Fleming and Russell Braddon
　(*b*) First R.N.A. Dinner. From left to right: John Attenborough, myself, A. P. Herbert, Alex Stuart, Bill Smith
8 (*a*) With Neill on holiday at Pollensa, Majorca
　(*b*) With Paul Hodder-Williams, the Chairman of Hodder and Stoughton, at an office party

FOREWORD

My father, Roland Pertwee, should have written the Foreword to this delightful autobiography but, alas, he died before it was complete. He and Denise were devoted friends for some forty years. They were so utterly different in outlook and temperament that many outsiders must have wondered what on earth they saw in one another—Roland, the loudly proclaimed cynic, Denise the unashamed romantic. In truth, Roland was incurably sentimental at heart, though nothing would have made him admit it. Denise, in her writing, may seem to view life through rose-tinted spectacles but her unhappy and loveless childhood has forged her into a woman of outstandingly strong character and wisdom, and has given her a sharp and penetrating wit which is more than a match for any man. Both, in their own way, admired and envied the other. Together they invariably brought out the best in the other.

I feel honoured and touched to have been asked to take my father's place in writing this introduction. My one regret is that I shall not do it half as well as he. My one justification is that I have known Denise all my life.

What is the secret of this astonishing woman's success? One hundred and sixty-six novels to date and many more, I assure the reader, to come. It is not, as some may assume, the result of an almost incredible mass production. It is not quantity that counts in this highly competitive field. By all normal standards Denise's public should have been gradually melting away over the years but, instead, it is actually growing. She is more successful today than she has ever been—and has thirteen grand-children!

There are, I think, two answers to my question. First, Denise not only *looks* quite extraordinarily young and attractive, but she *is* extraordinarily young both in mind and outlook. She can sit down with anyone of any age and can entrance and be entranced by them. She never longs for 'the good old days'. She is only interested in the present—and the future. It never occurs to her to *try* and keep abreast of the times. She is completely and naturally a part of these times. I have known and loved Denise since my childhood and, to me, she has never aged in any way. I have loved her because, even when I was very young, she treated me as an equal, as somebody who mattered and who might contribute something to her own knowledge of human nature.

From about the age of fifteen I was determined to be a writer but was acutely conscious that having a highly successful author as a father was liable to be a disadvantage. The majority of people to whom I confided my ambition would smile indulgently, pat my head and talk about the advantages of 'safer' professions. Not so Denise. Whatever her private feelings may have been, she offered me nothing but encouragement. It was she who gave me my very first literary assignment, if it can be called that. It was 'helping' her to answer readers' problems in a woman's weekly magazine. Psychologically—and I'll guarantee she knew it—this worked wonders with my morale. Apart from the joy of actually being *paid* something for my efforts (how much, is our secret), she even had the decency to use one of my suggested solutions to a highly complicated and embarrassing sexual problem sent in by a lady from Glasgow. A few months later, aged sixteen, I sat down and wrote my first, *very* romantic, short story which, to everyone's astonishment, was accepted by the *Windsor Magazine*.

The second answer to Denise's success lies in the single word 'Sincerity'. One need not be a mathematician to work out her quite amazing daily output over the past years. This one can admire and envy but it is no more than the application of a rigid daily discipline combined with God's gift of a constantly inventive mind. To these must be added the essential ingredient that Denise passionately *believes* in what she writes. Moreover, she wants to write better all the time. It is her firm determination that each new book must be better than the last. Hers is no routine chore to make money or to meet publisher's deadline. She would write even if there were no publisher to buy her material. Hers is a labour of love in every sense of the word.

What else can be said of Denise that the reader may not discover for himself from the pages of this book? She talks of her three daughters and her ever increasing brood of grandchildren. What she cannot, in modesty, mention is the type of mother that she has been. Her own unhappy childhood, with a father she scarcely knew and a mother who signally failed to provide that vital maternal interest and affection, has deeply affected her. She is *all* mother—devoted, generous, affectionate, possessive, adoring, critical and, above all, *interested*. Her passionate need to love and be loved which is so touchingly revealed in this book, is further illustrated in her intense interest in her children and grandchildren. Their problems are her problems. She could no more disassociate herself from them than she could give up writing. Denise works harder and longer than any writer that I know. She can relax and enjoy herself more fully than any hard worker that I know. She can seek with enthusiasm a host of other outlets— broadcasting, television, committees but, with all this, she still finds time to keep in close personal contact with every member of her family. Children at some time or another invariably resent too much parental interest in their affairs. No doubt in their younger, more mercurial years her daughters may have resisted some of her opinions but, today, I can think of no other family which is more closely or more affectionately linked.

I commend anyone to read this book whether or not they like romantic fiction. In this emancipated age of broken marriages, teenage promiscuity, of 'Mods' and 'Rockers' it is easy—and sometimes tempting—to raise a cheap laugh at the expense of the romantic novelist. It is said that they write unrealistic, sentimental mush; that they provide an opiate for simple minds; that they face no facts, draw no true picture of our world; that they are either fools or cynics.

I cannot speak for all romantic novelists but, certainly, with

Denise none of this is true. She is neither a cynic nor a fool. Make no mistake, she *knows* what life is all about. Readers of her autobiography will see that she had to learn this the hard way. Her novels reveal her own ardent wish that life *could* be different and more beautiful. She has always longed and will always long for a world in which True Love flourishes and endures.

Which one of us, in the deep recesses of our heart, does not wish the same?

Michael Pertwee,
34 Aylestone Ave.,
London, N.W.6.

PART ONE

1

FOR a long time I have resisted the temptation to write my life story. I have repeatedly been asked to do so. After all, it has been a full, exciting life and I have had two marriages; three daughters; and up to date, thirteen grandchildren—and written one hundred and sixty-six novels.

Many of my relatives and friends seem to think that it would be a pity if I didn't put on record a few of the strange things that have happened in my life. I shall tell the truth, 'the whole truth and nothing but the truth!'

I want people to believe that, fiction writer though I am by profession, I have no intention of allowing one fictitious word to enter this book. Neither shall I exaggerate. I will try to write without prejudice, if any human being can really do that!

When one is young, one loves or hates passionately, but with maturity, things fall more into their proper place. Yearnings, enthusiasms, fervent hopes or fears recede into the background —not altogether to vanish but to become like pictures one has once painted and which can later be examined with a calm, critical faculty that was non-existent at the time one was involved.

Everything of note that happens when one is young seems larger than life-size. Everything hurts terribly. Disillusionment is bitter. The loss of our illusions, the fading of our dreams, seem hard to bear.

Yet there comes a time when you can not only bear this pain, but smile, if a little sadly, at the memory of it.

I still feel capable of love, of warm deep feeling; not, I am glad to say, of hatred. It was love and romance that always dominated and directed my life.

What may surprise those who know my work, and who read this book, will be the fact that a romantic novelist like myself could have had such an unromantic beginning.

Once when recounting my past to my great friend, the late Roland Pertwee, novelist, playwright, author of some of England's finest short stories, he said:

'I find it strange that you should have been through these terrible things and suffered so many reverses, yet are able to write in such romantic vein. One might imagine from your novels that you had never known anything in your life but sweetness and romance.'

How wrong he was! I was born 'a romantic' but for a long time those who had charge of me did about everything possible to knock romance out of me. If my story disappoints readers who would have preferred it otherwise, I am sorry, but I must tell the truth.

How much in a person's nature, apart from physical appearance, is inherited? Can such traits ever really be erased? Are they less important than environment? These are problems that have always fascinated me. It is of course as difficult to remember things selectively as in sequence. Memories are fleeting, and a moment can be of vastly more importance than a year, but of one thing I am certain, that right from the beginning, my attitude to love has only been an extension of my attitude to life.

2

I SHALL begin with my father, Herman Klein. He was born at Norwich on the 23rd July, 1856—one of eight brothers, each of whom eventually achieved distinction in one or other of the arts.

The Kleins were a talented family. My grandfather, a violinist, originally came over to England from Mitau on the Baltic and married an Alsacienne—a clever rather dominating woman. My paternal grandmother spoke and taught seven languages. Once in England my grandfather became a dancing instructor—the whole family played some kind of musical instrument and sang, or wrote for a living.

Father was the eldest son. He was educated at Norwich Grammar School and studied singing under the famous teacher, Manuel Garcia.

The Kleins had no money. All the boys had to start at the bottom of the ladder.

Father at once proved himself to be of remarkable talent. He could act, he could play the piano, he could write. He was an ardent student of the classics, had a good voice and with all these talents, also had tremendous driving force. It was to carry him a long way without material help from others.

When he was only twenty-two, he composed a special Grand March for the opening of the Paris Exhibition. This was dedicated by special permission to His Royal Highness, the Prince of Wales. From that day onward, Father rose to fame.

For reasons which I shall describe later on, I did not see much of my Father. My memories of him are of a short rather squarely built man with piercing hazel-green eyes, handsome features and tremendous charm.

Because of his obsession with his work, he made a poor family man. Certainly, out of his three marriages, only one was a success and that was the last.

He was a man with many facets to his character—he was not only an artist but a sportsman. He loved tennis and played it moderately well until he was well over seventy. He also adored cricket. His greatest joy was to watch the big matches at Lord's. He was a member there and chose Avenue Road, St. John's Wood, for his final home for the express purpose of being close to the famous cricket-ground.

This, then, was my father.

Now what of my mother whom he met and married in the year 1890?

3

MOTHER was a very different character.

An Australian, she was born on the 11th March, 1872, in a house on Emerald Hill, Victoria. She was the youngest of ten children.

My grandfather, George Chesterton Cornwell, had emigrated from Cambridge which was his original home and married a beautiful millionaire debutante named Jemima Redpath.

Grandfather had just floated a gold mine—the first of several. But what he made he lost again. He was a born gambler—either very rich or very poor. I regret to say that he ended in extreme poverty. He was adventuresome but careless.

My mother, christened Kathleen Clarice Louise, was destined to spend an unhappy girlhood after the death at an early age of her own mother. Her sister, Frances, who was ten years older than herself, had just married a promising young man named George Hutchinson (he was destined to become Sir George Hutchinson, founder of one of the biggest publishing houses in Great Britain). The new married couple decided to return to England. They took my mother with them. She was a lonely child although her sister and brother-in-law did what they could to make her happy.

Another yet older sister married round about the same time and left Melbourne for England. My Aunt Alice proved to be one of the most remarkable of women; she was the mother of the famous journalist and theatrical producer, Sydney Carroll.

When mother was sixteen, Aunt Alice (then Mrs. Robinson), a woman with as much mental energy, charm and lack of providence as Grandfather, became the proprietor of *The Sunday Times*. This, she soon sold to Gomer Berry. It always seems fantastic to me to think that my aunt owned such a paper and passed it on for what must have been a 'mere song' to the Berry Brothers (one of whom later became Lord Camrose).

Those who remember tell me that when mother was sixteen

she was utterly fascinating. She had enormous blue eyes, dark curly hair, a retroussé nose and an engaging way of looking through her lashes. She played the piano, sang sentimental songs with more charm than talent and could write a little. (In years to come she was to earn her living with her pen.) Everybody fell in love with her. Among them my father who met her at a dinner party given by Aunt Alice who was then employing him as the music critic on her Sunday paper.

It was love at first sight for Father. He needed a wife and he found my mother irresistible although he was thirty-four—she only ten years older than his own daughter, Sibyl. For Mother, the affair was doomed from the start. He was too old for her and by nature too cold and intellectual. She, although quick-witted, was not the student type. She was imbued with Victorian sentimentality. She wanted romance and all the attention that had so far been denied her. I'm afraid she did not find this with my father.

They were married in London. All that I know about their early days has been told to me by Mother, and she was prejudiced. She loathed my father from the honeymoon onwards; and when a soft, sweet, romantic woman begins to hate a man she really *does* hate; nobody can be harder or more cruel.

The honeymoon was described to me as a disaster. I cannot say it sounds attractive from mother's point of view. Father was first and foremost an egotist. He was fond of climbing. He took my mother to Switzerland and, according to her, went out climbing mountains all day, while she hung miserably round the hotel waiting for his return. What she had visualised from a husband was adoration, tenderness and, above all, admiration. She was naturally vain. She received no tenderness from him. She said that all Father, a Victorian autocrat, seemed to want to do was to claim his marital rights.

Resentment and disappointment became in time a festering sore within Mother. She found if difficult, too, at her young age to look after Sibyl. So she, poor child, was sent abroad to various boarding schools where she remained for the next ten years.

My parents settled in London in Temple Chambers. There,

17

Father established himself as a teacher of singing and there, my first brother, Adrian, was born; the son who was in time to become distinguished in the fields of art, science and photography.

For a short time Mother was happier but still at loggerheads with Father. He was fast climbing the ladder of success. He was ambitious. He loved the limelight and he wanted Mother to entertain for him. If he was no great lover, he was at least proud of her attractions as a woman, and pleased when some of the great men of the day fell in love with her—so long as they kept their distance!

My brother Adrian was handed over to a Nanny. Mother was forced to give parties for Father, and accompany him to most of the operas during the season, or to concerts, listening to music that bored her unutterably. She only liked one or two of the more emotional operas by Wagner or Puccini. She yawned her way through music by Bach, Mozart or Beethoven which to my father was food and drink.

Incidentally, one of the most touching mementos that I possess of him is a big worn leather-bound book of Mozart's works given to him in his early boyhood. On the fly-leaf he had written these words: 'Once I was poor, now I am rich.' But to mother there was no richness to be found in any of the tremendous works by the great composers. They left her chilled.

After the birth of my brother, Daryl, two years later, the relationship between my parents worsened. Father remained immersed in his work. Mother grew a little harder, but never lost the youthfulness of that baby face, the touch of coquetry that made her so attractive. She was entirely faithful to my father, but had her admirers—one of them a famous stockbroker of the day who made pocket-money for her on the Stock Exchange. Soon she bought a brougham, was also to be seen riding in the Row. She was a fine horsewoman.

In time my parents moved to No. 4 Whitehall Court where they occupied a ground-floor flat. There, Father had his studio, and Mother held musical At Homes.

It was there that I was born, on the 1st February in the year

1897 (Queen Victoria's Diamond Jubilee!).

I was told by my mother that I was a result of a 'reconciliation' between herself and Father. They had had one of their innumerable rows just before Father went over to America where his brother Charles was living. On his return, he and Mother had some kind of *rapprochement*. Thus, I was launched into the world.

When I was laid in my cot apparently the doctor leaned over me and noticed that I gave him a saucy look. He shook his head and said to my mother:

'I fear your pretty little daughter is going to be a flirt.'

At the time, being only an hour or two old, I was scarcely able to retort as I would have wished:

'*Hardly surprising*, doc, when you think of Mama!'

My father was supposed to have been pleased that his third child was a little girl, but Mother says that he went to sleep while she was in labour and gave orders not to be disturbed even after the birth. He paid scant attention to me and continued to neglect his pretty young wife while he carried on with his career.

One is so often asked at what age one begins to remember things. My first memory goes back to three years old. I was taken late one afternoon by my nurse, Miss Love ('Nanna' we called her) to peep through the open door of my father's studio. He was holding a party. A little man with a shock of white hair sat on the stool at the Steinway performing 'fireworks' up and down the keys. At least that was what it sounded like to me. He finished to a burst of applause. Nanna whispered to me:

'You must always remember this, my dearie. You have seen and heard the great Mr. Paderewski playing.'

I never did forget the little genius or any of the other great musicians or singers who came to father's studio during those early years.

At the age of four, I once overheard an argument in which my father said in a loud voice:

'I consider that to be a very generous salary.'

When next we had celery with the cheese course I proudly

presented a stalk to my father and told him that it was a 'generous celery' which absurdity he neither understood nor appreciated. Nothing that I ever said or did as a child was applauded or recorded. My parents had no time for such trivialities. They were too obsessed with themselves and their own lives.

Soon we moved from Whitehall Court to one of those beautiful Nash houses in Regent's Park—No 34 Chester Terrace. It was a magnificent home where my mother had her own personal maid, Louise; a good chef, and the usual bevy of servants that were kept in those days by well-to-do families. She had everything she wanted, within reason. My brothers and I were kept firmly upstairs in the nurseries.

After we moved to Chester Terrace, I played happily with my toys little dreaming that my parents' marriage was drawing to an unhappy close.

Vaguely, I recall the day in January when Queen Victoria died—the black crêpe, muffled streets and the weeping. We watched the funeral procession from our nursery window. Nanna was pleased when my two brothers and I cried as a tribute to the good, kind old Queen. But I would have wept a great deal harder had I guessed what lay in store for me in the future. For in 1901 my mother left the house in Regent's Park never to return. Still only thirty, she had grown restless and unable to live without romance. She went to a party, met and fell madly in love with a young, handsome army officer. He became infatuated with her. I can tell from old photographs how fascinating she must have been, with her enormous eyes, curly hair piled high upon her head, slim figure attired in a long swirling skirt and lace blouse with leg o' mutton sleeves.

She had Irish ancestry on her mother's side. Hence that rather haunting Irish kind of attraction. She had exquisite hands with long slender fingers and oval nails which have been inherited by my brother Adrian's daughter, Silvia. Unfortunately for me I have Father's small square hands with strong 'musician's fingers'. I am physically like him altogether. My brothers favoured our mother. I remember little else of her at that time. I was hardly ever with her. But I can recall one

20

other episode when I was about four years old.

I was being driven down to Esher by my Aunt Alice in her carriage and pair. As we approached the gates of her home the horses bolted. The carriage overturned. The horses were pulled in by the groom. My aunt, who was a bulky woman, tried to shield me with her own body and succeeded, but ricked her back in so doing. I remember screaming until a coachman bent over me and said:

'For God's sake, Missie, don't make that noise or the horses will bolt again.'

I obviously must have stopped screaming, because they stood still, puffing and panting, and I was pulled out unhurt except for a few minor bruises.

4

I WAS four when my mother fastened her desperate affections upon this young army officer who was to change her destiny. Herbert Arthur Berkeley Dealtry, Second Lieutenant in the 10th Worcesters, was one of the four sons of an Esher family (they were a rather snobbish aristocratic lot). The other sons were also in the Army. They were horrified by the liaison between Berkeley and a married woman older than himself. It must be remembered that at the turn of the century it was an appalling disgrace to be involved in a divorce. Drawing-room doors were shut upon both the respondent and co-respondent.

When we discussed the affair later in life, my mother assured me that she did not wish to leave her children, but was forced into it because she could no longer bear life with my father. In spite of the pomp and luxury of her life as the wife of a famous music critic who was received in all the London drawing-rooms and patronised by royalty, she was desperately unhappy. She flung herself into Berkeley's arms and considered the world well lost for love.

Eventually she eloped with him. They reached Brindisi and

there she was pursued by Father and Aunt Alice both of whom tried to induce her to return. My father no longer loved my mother but he wanted her back. His pride was injured and it was a singularly unfortunate thing for him that this was the second wife to leave him. It was not going to look good in the eyes of the world if another divorce became public, he said. Mother flatly refused to go back to him. He held it against her permanently that she ruined his life, for after the scandal of the divorce he was forced to leave England and start a new life in America. This meant an almost entirely fresh career. He had to leave all his triumphs and important contacts in business and society behind him.

Mother told me that after she returned to London she used to go into Regent's Park to try and catch a glimpse of us children. She was forbidden to visit us. She says she pined for us, but Berkeley came first. There was no doubt that she was really in love with him and remained so during the fourteen years of their marriage.

It was bad luck on Father and on Sibyl who, being nineteen years old when mother left father, found herself having to take charge of three small children for whom she had no particular liking. She had always been exceedingly jealous of me—the second girl in the family—so I was fated to receive scant affection from her.

Like all children in those days I was, of course, kept in the nursery with Nanna. It was she who kissed and comforted me, but unfortunately she was taken ill and went away to hospital immediately after my mother left. During the following week I had a nasty accident.

A nursemaid took me for a walk in Regent's Park. I ran ahead, tripped, fell down and fractured my arm. I have since proved to be one of those unfortunate people who are 'accident-prone'.

I remember my own frantic yells as I was rushed back to Chester Terrace, but there was now no Mother to dry my tears. Sister Sibyl found it all an added worry. Father was solicitous when he saw me but that was rarely. However I enjoyed being, on occasions, the centre of attraction. The arm unfortunately was incorrectly set and very painful.

I can remember lying awake that night crying. Suddenly someone lit the gas. I sat up. I saw beside my cot a beautiful woman in a glittering evening gown holding a glass of champagne in her hand. My father was standing beside her. They were smiling down at me.

She was Madame Nordica, one of father's most famous pupils and friends and a famous Wagnerian singer of the period. She knew, of course, that my mother had eloped and was no longer in the house. Being a kindly woman, she had asked to be allowed to see 'the poor baby'. For once my father was induced to make a pet of me. Nordica wrapped a shawl around me. I was carried down to the studio where a party of father's musician friends had gathered for a *soirée*.

I can remember the other women 'ooh-ing' and 'ah-ing' over the little girl whose arm was in a splint.

Somebody gave me a piece of cake. Somebody else lifted a champagne goblet to my lips but I spat it out. (I have been spitting it out ever since!) I have never cared for alcohol. It does not suit me. My father was an abstemious man and took only a little wine occasionally with his dinner. But he loved good food (so do I), prided himself on his carving and made a positive ritual of mixing the salad-dressing.

My arm grew worse instead of better. Not only did I suffer excruciatingly when I was on board *The Philadelphia*, the ship that took us all to America a few weeks later; but the arm had to be reset. The New York specialist saw me, pulled the arm a little further and further every day until the bone snapped again. There was no question of anaesthetic. I remember plainly a bearded gentleman with a monocle on a black tape, leaning over me, patting my head, saying I was a brave girl and giving me a chocolate, but I still bear the scar of the fracture—the two bits of bone came right through the flesh.

Both my arms bear scars. There is also one on my left arm. When I was six, a small boy of the same age dug his penknife into it and I was proud of the way I bled, but he cried more than I did. I had to have sixteen stitches.

I can remember no dramatic farewells on the day Mother

23

actually left home, only of being taken by Nanna to say good-night to her while she was dressing for the last reception she ever attended with Father. Mr. Truefitt, one of the great hair-dressers of her day, was there in person, curling my mother's long dark tresses with his tongs. I watched this in awe. He placed the tongs on a little spirit stove to reheat them and I felt the warmth against my face. Then he twisted a strand of her long hair with them and I let out a piercing scream. I thought he was going to burn her. My solicitude was mis-understood. Nanna was told to take me back to the nursery.

I remember little about the actual days that followed my mother's departure from Chester Terrace. It was whispered as a shameful thing. Then, by order from my father, I was told brutally that my mother had died and that I would never see her again. I don't think I cared over-much at the time. She had become a stranger to me.

The lease of the house in Chester Terrace was put up for sale.

A few nights before we left, a pipe burst and the drawing-room ceiling gave way. I was taken by a maid to see the big holes and the torn plaster and paper on the floor.

It was my final memory before leaving England.

5

WHAT with sea-sickness and my broken arm, the voyage from Southampton to New York was a nightmare for me. No doubt it was also unpleasant for my half-sister.

She was a highly strung, handsome girl with raven dark hair and large brown eyes. She spoke four languages, played the piano, sang and acted. She was entirely self-centred. I can imagine now that she must have felt it hard that she had to take on the burden of looking after us children as well as father.

I cried miserably all through the voyage and kept Sibyl

awake, which was unpopular. My arm tortured me.

Sibyl snapped at me continually; only the stewardess was sympathetic.

I rarely saw my father. There were one or two well-known men in the music world on board. He spent most of his time with them. He could scarcely be called an affectionate parent. He was a disappointed man embittered by my mother's conduct.

We arrived in New York and were taken at once to a tall, bleak-looking house in West 77th Street. It was the home of my Uncle, Charles Klein. By then he had become an American citizen. He was hard working, ambitious and a talented dramatist. His wife Lilian, a fervent Christian Scientist, had agreed to give us children a home. Uncle Charles, always a warm-hearted and kindly little man, was only too delighted to have his brother in the house and to help him establish himself as a music critic and singing master in the new country.

For me there was scant welcome. The boys were attractive and good-looking. Adrian showed signs of becoming a gifted artist. Daryl was sweet and tractable. They seemed to offer few problems. I was a little girl not yet five and difficult to manage. I was both a responsibility and a bore to my aunt. She had a son of her own—Philip. My brothers could be educated with him—but what to do with me seemed a problem she did not want to try and solve.

I spent the next few months of my life in a room at the top of the tall house in charge of a servant named Hattie. I remember her to this day, because she was kind to me and often took me down to the basement kitchen where I became a great favourite with all the staff. At least I felt welcome by them.

Photographs show me as a small child with flowing chestnut hair and curiously sad eyes for one so young. I flung myself into acting for Aunt Lilian's servants. The cook used to put me on top of the big wooden kitchen table and I dressed up and entertained them. They roared with laughter and declared that 'Miss Denise *must* be put on the stage!'

In the kitchen, however, my popularity began and ended. Aunt Lilian was too busy entertaining for her husband to have time for me. She was not particularly pleased to have my father in her house, anyhow. He filled it with music, singing and his pupils. There were frequent family disagreements.

From the start I seemed to annoy my aunt. I was neither tractable nor 'cuddly'. I had a strong will and an enquiring mind. I can quite well see what a pest I must have been with my continuous 'Why's?' and 'Why-nots?'

Sibyl had settled down and was busily training for the New York stage. My father began to find me such an embarrassment that he wished he had left me in England with my mother.

Mother, as far as I knew, was dead. I had no one upon whom to fasten my affections; in fact the only person in that New York house whom I remember with any tenderness was Uncle Charles. He seemed more human and kindly than the others. He used to let me come and sit on a hassock at his feet while he played his cello, which was his hobby. He often pleaded that I should not be punished so unnecessarily by Aunt Lilian or Sibyl.

The religious fervour which held Aunt Lilian in such a thrall at that time had repercussions upon me. She wanted to turn me into a Christian Scientist. She had already converted my father. It is in its way an excellent but hard religion and it produces a certain austerity and harshness of character. Many times when I fell down or hurt myself I was told to stop crying immediately because 'there is no pain, only evil'. In theory this may well be true, but in practice, no small child could take it!

One day I developed pneumonia. My aunt called in a Christian Scientist healer but I nearly died, so they hastily included a doctor, which was just as well or I wouldn't be writing my autobiography today!

Uncle Charles owned a country house outside New York. I remember one or two pleasant summer days there, and also an unpleasant one when my brothers, my cousin Philip and my half-sister took me out in a boat on a lake and threw me into the water. They believed that was the best way to make a child swim.

26

I thought I would drown, but I did learn to swim—for my life!

As time went by, my aunt began to despair of me. I was too naughty, often disobedient and, on the surface, I seemed to lack affection. It was because nobody showed me any. Nobody wanted to kiss me so I didn't offer kisses. I became self-centred, and perhaps with the seeds of the romantic writer already growing within me, began to make up stories which I told to other children when given the chance. My aunt told my father that she feared I was untruthful. I did lie at times—out of fear and a distorted imagination. To me, already, fantasy was fact. I lived in a world of my own.

I was sent by my aunt and father to my first boarding school. Aunt Lilian cannot altogether be blamed. She did what she thought was best for me. She chose a school in Flushing, run by a woman who was also a Christian Scientist. She was humourless and a harsh disciplinarian. My aunt liked her; it was considered that I needed discipline.

I do not remember the name of this woman who became my headmistress. To me she was just a cold-blooded devil. Once again I made myself unpopular. I was too adventuresome and high-spirited for her. She did not want an enquiring mind. She preferred her pupils to be docile and easy-to-manage.

When I found that I was not to be allowed to develop mentally, I grew even more secretive. Then they called me sly. I was full of ideas. I adored 'make-believe'. The 'head' discouraged this. She had had her orders from my aunt and half-sister. If I became too recalcitrant, I was to be whipped.

No doubt my relatives had little idea of the consequences. The headmistress, unknown to anybody at the time, had a tumour on the brain. Very slowly she was going insane. She fastened her unnatural hatred upon me.

She was a sadist. She hung a small length of rope above my bed and kept it there so I could see it, daily. Whether I was good or bad I was to be reminded that if I broke the rules the rope would be used to beat me with. A charming idea! If I had been less strong-minded I might have gone under—never recovered psychologically—but threats and cruelties seemed somehow to increase my powers of resistance.

I tried rather hopelessly to be good so as to avoid the thrashings. They seemed to me to be for things that I hadn't done, or for such minor offences they did not deserve punishment.

I learned, gradually, to keep my ideas and fantasies to myself. The half-crazy woman who held my fate between her hands seemed, however, determined to take a gross delight in bullying me.

Such was my father's amazing coldness of heart that I understand now why my mother, who was so much warmer and more sentimental, hated him.

After a while he decided that it would be best to remove me from Aunt Lilian's care. He made a grave decision; he wrote to my mother and asked if she would like to have me back.

By that time, mother had been married for over three years. to her beloved Berkeley. They were very hard up, living, at the time they received this letter from New York, in a furnished cottage in Sussex—Five Ashes, near Mayfield.

Mother had despaired of ever being allowed to see any of her three children again. Later she told me that my father's offer filled her with joy. It was a joy that lasted only a short time. My step-father did not want me. I think he foresaw that the introduction of the child of the first marriage into *his* married life might be disastrous. However, he told mother that if she wanted her little daughter—she must have her.

Now, in New York, I was coolly informed that my mother was not dead but alive, and that I was to travel to England on a big liner to join her. A booking was made for me and a stewardness detailed to look after me until we reached Southampton.

I had entirely forgotten my mother's existence. It is rather a grim thought that her amazing 'resuscitation' made little impression on me. I had grown used to being handed from one person and one place to another. It did not seem to matter. The one thing that those three years in America *had* done was to set up a kind of indifference in me—an immunity to either joy or sorrow. I was always impressionable, however, and had, like all the Kleins in New York, become a Christian Scientist.

28

I did not understand the religion, but I was a born mimic and like a parrot I could quote long passages from *Science & Health* by Mary Baker G. Eddy.

I was told by my aunt, and Uncle Charles, to try to convert my mother once I got back to her. To this I was quite agreeable. It gave me a feeling of importance. At last I had a mission.

What I did not know was that when I kissed my two brothers goodbye I would not see them again for many long years.

6

My mother had signed a legal document accepting full custody of me with no financial help from her first husband, and there was to be no question of his ever seeing me again. He had just contracted his third marriage to a beautiful Bostonian —Hélène Hathaway. He still had my brothers to educate and I think he imagined that my step-father, having wronged him, should be the one to provide the wherewithal for *my* education. How wrong he was about *that*!

It was agreed in this rather disgraceful document, signed by both my parents, that I could see my brothers but only by mutual arrangement in the distant future. The boys were brought up in New York and did not return to England until 1909 and even then were systematically prevented from visiting me. Their wealthy, sociable step-mother made life more agreeable for them as they grew older, but I hold it against Hélène that it was she who made it a condition of her marriage to Father that I should be for ever banished.

On the voyage back to England, I shared a cabin (on the *Kaiser-Wilhelm II*) with a lady who was travelling alone. I had no idea that this same ship carried my father and his newly-made wife on their honeymoon. They were in a different part of the liner. They saw me only once or twice. I was, as usual, very much *de trop*.

Hélène appears to have been the one who understood and appreciated Father with far greater feeling and loyalty than his first two wives. She was also a woman of means and generously enabled my father when he was hard up, to carry on with his career in America.

Mr. Harris, my mother's solicitor, met the ship at Southampton. My father handed me over to him rather as he would a legal document. The third Mrs. Klein was only too anxious to be rid of the *enfant-terrible*. Off I trotted beside Mr. Harris and was taken down to Sussex to my unknown mother and step-father—and yet another new life!

I craved for love, yet it is a curious thing that at seven years old I seemed incapable of showing any sign of it. I suppose if a child receives no tenderness for a long time it learns to exist without it. I had retired into a shell. Mother was no 'child psychologist' and did not look beneath the surface for the real ME. As soon as she saw me she was to utter those words which I heard repeated again and again during the ensuing years—always with bitterness.

'Oh dear—*just* like your father!'

My step-father agreed—the lawyer, too. Nobody seemed pleased.

I do not think it was my physical likeness to father, but my nature—the mannerisms which I had inherited—that offended mother. She remembered only his faults. After all, he had not shown *her* much pity or understanding. Nobody excused me for inheriting my father's characteristics. No one had the patience to help me over the various stiles as I grew older. I had either to voice my opinions rather forcibly or not be heard at all.

Mother believed she had really wanted her daughter back. But it was my brother, Adrian—her elder son—whom she had loved. Not her difficult little Denise.

For the first time in her life she was blissfully happy. My step-father worshipped her. She received all the petting and passionate love she had been denied by Father. Berkeley was an ideal lover, well-read, intelligent and a charming companion. But he was also rather weak and easily led. Having broken with his own family because of the divorce, and having resigned his commission, he was penniless. He could not keep himself, let alone a wife. He could only try to make her happy. But they were facing penury when I returned to them.

Mother had already begun to show her remarkable qualities of courage and adaptability. She had a talent for writing. Once married to Berkeley, she began to find a market for her romantic little stories.

My step-father typed them. But it was mother who was the real bread-winner. Bad for his character! She then found she had to keep me as well. But she was quite happy. She and Berkeley lived in a world of their own in which I was not included—despite her efforts to care for me.

She began to try to foster in me her own hatred of my father. She paid him only one grudging compliment. He was a wonderful worker, she said. He had achieved, unaided, a position of distinction in his particular field; but I grew up to believe that he was entirely to blame for the break-up of the marriage.

Mother decided that I should no longer be known by the hateful name of 'Klein'. So, 'Denise Dealtry' I became, and was later married under this name. I was told to address Berkeley as 'Daddy' and gradually I did, indeed, grow to look upon him as a father.

As time went by, I became my mother's most devout follower and I longed for my love to be returned; but when I say that she always did her duty by me to the full and paid for my education—that is as far as it went while I was young. She could not love me any more than she had loved my father. This poisoned our relationship but I realise now how hard it must have been for her to feel real affection for me. She had had so many disappointments and I unwittingly turned out to be one of the worst. In the end, even her life with Berkeley failed to be the perfect partnership for which she had hoped. She was singularly unlucky.

What really spoilt her relationship with me, her daughter, was jealousy. Her love for my step-father was an obsession,

31

and I was a constant thorn in her flesh.

Until I was eight or nine years old, things ran comparatively smoothly. She did not mind him being either kind or attentive to me. He was both those things. I remember him as a genial happy-go-lucky fellow—too happy-go-lucky, unfortunately, for he never managed to find a job, and only earned a few pounds for writing occasional magazine stories under a pseudonym. But he was not successful. It was mother who earned the living, often under the most trying circumstances during the years that followed my return to her. I remember all her efforts, and the way she educated me, with huge admiration. I admired, too, the fortitude she always showed in pain, for she had poor health and suffered a lot during the last years of her life. She rarely complained.

On the day that the solicitor handed me over to her, she was still young and beautiful. She had said goodbye to her life as a London socialite—to the world of music—and to the circle of great singers in which she used to move. She did not seem to care. She was anti-social. She wanted to segregate herself and her new husband from the world. In any case, as their finances were so bad they could not afford London life. They were still 'disgraced' in the eyes of a society which had not yet ceased to be smug and censorious, and to persecute those who offended the popular conception of 'strict morality'. (A condition which was to continue until the guns of the First World War thundered across Europe and wiped out so much smugness and hypocrisy.)

They had temporarily taken a furnished cottage in Mayfield and it was there I arrived with my small trunk full of clothes and little else. My first night with my newly-found mother and step-father must have been more of an astonishment and a revelation to them that it was to me. I remember it only vaguely. But when I was older they often told me how, when they went upstairs to say goodnight to me, I stood up in my bed in my long white nightdress and delivered a homily on Christian Science which, apparently, reduced them both to speechlessness. I repeated like a parrot what I had heard from my New York teachers—without comprehension. My new

32

'Daddy' who had a sense of humour told me in years to come that it was that absurd childish effort to convert two sinners that decided my mother that she had made a mistake in taking me back. It filled her with dismay. I was not going to be the little daughter she longed for. I was no sweet little dumpling with tears in eyes and thumb in mouth, begging to be cuddled. I might have been an interesting child, but I was not particularly lovable. I had become far too precocious. Mother was not amused.

Berkeley, however, tried to further my education at home. To him, I owe much of my knowledge of books and history. He accumulated a large library in time and I read, particularly, all the classics that mother never cared for. However her taste in novels by writers like Ethel M. Dell was eventually to be useful. I read light romances, too, and became interested in the technique.

Berkeley tried in vain to get a job. His mother was dead. He had no relatives to help us. Adrian, his brother, who was kind and generous to all, was busy making his own way in life. Cosmo, young and handsome and the most endearing of my step-uncles, was unable to do a thing for Berkeley.

There was absolutely no help for the young couple who now had a seven-year-old child on their hands. Then one day a friend suggested there was money to be made out of oranges in California.

For a year, Mother and 'Daddy' toyed with the idea of trying to raise enough money for a journey to California.

In the meantime we moved from Sussex to a tiny cottage called 'Morfa' in Porth on the north coast of Cornwall. Porth then was an isolated village—with one post office and a few other cottages besides ours. There was little to be seen on the beach save the seagulls and the puffins. Today Porth is a popular resort crowded in summer with people, caravans and bungalows; all peace and beauty destroyed.

In the village of St. Columb Minor there lived an old woman named Elsie Evans who was once mother's cook-general, and who did all the work of the house and cooking for one pound a week.

I visited her a year ago.

She had a few interesting remarks to make about the past.

'I adored Mrs. Dealtry. She was a sweet, pretty thing and Mr. Dealtry, so handsome. They two was crazily in love, but you was just a poor lil ole maid, lonesome—always in trouble. Elsie played noughts and crosses with you in her kitchen, and took you for walks. She loved you, and she'm proud to see in the papers how her lil ole maid has become a famous writer!'

Well—the 'lonesome lil ole maid' remembers old Cornish Elsie with affection. She looked after me and loved me.

While we were living in Porth, Adrian decided to be friendly with his young brother again, despite the disapproval of the divorce. He came to stay with us in Cornwall. Mother disliked him, but he was a fine man. He had none of Berkeley's fascination for women, nor did he ever marry. He spent most of his life in Mexico where he lived and worked for the Mexican Light and Power Company.

He was more understanding of me and my needs than the other two. Night after night he would take me on his knee and tell me wonderful stories. When he left Porth I wept bitterly, although I think Mother was relieved to be alone once more with her husband.

I was to see Uncle Adrian again sooner than I imagined, because Daddy at last decided to accept an offer to work for a firm of orange-growers in Los Angeles.

Uncle Adrian had it in mind at first to join Berkeley in buying an orange grove; but that was not to be. However, Mother and Daddy sold up our Cornish home and we travelled out on a slow, cheap boat to New York. Uncle Adrian travelled with us.

This must have been a tremendous adventure for mother. It was the beginning of many others, which ended in disaster for her. It was at times like these that she was at her best. Old Mrs. Dealtry had bitterly called her 'a raw Colonial' when she stole Berkeley from his family but it was that fighting Colonial spirit which came to mother's aid whenever she was faced with misfortune. She was very practical and really quite domesticated at heart. The one thing that really mattered to her was

34

that her Berkeley should find a job which would not part him from her, and so regain the self-respect he was losing by allowing her to be the sole bread-winner.

Although I was only eight years old, memories of that journey across the Atlantic and then on to California are still vivid. The experiences I went through were so varied and colourful that anybody might be excused for thinking that what I am about to write cannot be true. But as the title states, truth is often decidedly stranger than fiction!

7

MOTHER and Daddy had only a few hundred pounds behind them at the time we left England. We were forced to travel 'on the cheap'. Mother, used though she was to luxury, accepted her new hard life without complaint. Nothing mattered to her so long as my step-father was with her.

Just before we left Cornwall she had written a play—something she had always wanted to do, although she never lived to see any of her dramas produced. A London agent had shown interest in her last effort and sent it to his New York contact—none other than famous Mrs. de Mille—mother of Cecil B. de Mille whose name was to be associated in the future with so many Hollywood triumphs. She also happened to be my Uncle Charles's literary agent.

Mrs. de Mille had filled my mother with hope by suggesting a meeting once she reached New York. Nothing if not an optimist, Mother firmly believed this would lead to fame and fortune.

The voyage was uneventful. Once in New York (I had almost forgotten my early years there in Uncle Charlie's house), we went to our hotel. A bitter blow awaited my mother. A blow struck with unbelievable cruelty by both my father and uncle. Mrs. de Mille had told the latter about this proposed play Mother had written under the name of Kit Dealtry.

When Uncle Charles heard about it, he told my father. Father remembered my mother with a curious malevolence which was only to be matched by hers towards him, and he was furious because she and her new husband had come to America.

Mrs. de Mille was at once informed that if she handled Mrs. Dealtry's play or helped her (or Mr. Dealtry) in any way, Charles Klein would remove his patronage.

No agent could afford to lose such a client as the man who, after his successful play *The Music Master* was fast becoming famous in America. She did not wish to offend the Kleins.

Anyhow, my poor mother read the letter that awaited her and realised that her play had been returned. She sat down and cried heart-brokenly. This quite understandably roused her to fresh hatred of my father. Berkeley, too, seethed with indignation on her behalf. They told me that my father was a monster and encouraged me to think of him as such during the ensuing years.

Now the old problem reared its head.

'What do we do with Denise?'

I had had no regular or proper schooling. I could only read and write. But although education was not compulsory in the early nineteen-hundreds my mother knew that I should now receive some form of real education. They decided to send me to a convent in California as soon as we got there. Our future looked grim again. Now that the famous play was not to be put on the New York boards, our whole future depended upon what my step-father could make in the orange trade.

We travelled by train to Los Angeles; a week's journey in those days across the desert through Chicago—and over the border.

To me it was all exciting and wonderful. Mother and Daddy had no trouble with me then because I was interested and occupied—but they had plenty themselves.

The train broke down and arrived four hours late in Chicago.

There was no restaurant-car; the passengers were famished. We were given an hour's grace in a station buffet where in fact

36

we could order a grill. I remember how good our steaks tasted!

In Los Angeles we were met by Daddy's friend who had found the job for him. He was a good-natured American. Like all of them out there, he called my step-father 'Burkley Deeltry' and refused to do otherwise. It should, of course, have been pronounced in the English way ('Barcley Dawltry'). Everybody made Mother and Daddy welcome and I was petted and admired.

We were driven in an ancient Ford over a rough road to our bungalow. In those days, Los Angeles was still a small, sleepy town. It had not yet risen to magnificence under the fantastic banner of Hollywood. There *was* no Hollywood then.

The countryside was all made beautiful by the glorious sunshine. Mother fell in love with that climate, the beautiful orange-groves and the flowers.

Frankly, I do not remember much that happened during the year that followed our arrival, beyond the fact that I went to school. It was to day school at first—then I became a boarder in a Los Angeles convent.

We had no servants. Mother cooked and did everything. Daddy cheerfully tackled his new job—not a very well paid or progressive one, unfortunately. He was helping to pick oranges for export.

My Uncle Adrian Dealtry, whom we saw in California to begin with, decided not to join forces with Daddy and took himself off to Mexico. Soon Daddy grew tired of the orange-groves. A new American friend with more money seemed to admire the attractive, amusing Englishman (and, of course, his pretty wife). He offered Daddy a job that had better prospects, in an estate agent's office in San Diego.

Once again we packed up and moved (we were to move perpetually!). By this time, I was a seasoned traveller. I was also on better terms with Mother, and Daddy had become quite fond of me. There was quite a pleasant atmosphere in our bungalow and as long as I did not argue with or disobey my mother, all was well. She was extraordinarily strict with me.

During the next few months our living conditions improved. Daddy sold land. There was plenty of it to sell; hundreds of miles in those days, as yet undeveloped and going 'for a song'. Those same acres must today be worth a king's ransom.

We had a fair-sized bungalow with a wide verandah close to the sea-shore, a few miles out of San Diego.

Ocean Beach was a lonely place. There were only three or four bungalows beside our own, facing the sandy dunes and long blue line of breakers. Today, Ocean Beach is a huge, popular seaside resort.

I was nine years old on the 1st February, 1906.

Two months later, on the 18th April, the most terrible earthquake ever experienced on the west coast of California laid San Francisco flat.

We felt the repercussions even as far away as Ocean Beach. That same evening our bungalow began to shake. The ornamental china plates that mother kept on a high shelf fell off and were smashed. Daddy grabbed my hand, called for Mother and we all rushed out into the garden.

We stayed there, the earth trembling under us, and wondered for a moment what was going to happen next. The wind blew violently for an hour or two, then all was still; the bungalow stood firm. We were able to go inside again.

A telephone call came through later that night from a friend that Daddy had made in the estate agency business. He was in 'Frisco. He told Daddy that he had been staying in a hotel in the centre of the city and escaped just before it collapsed. He asked if we would give him shelter if he came to us.

He arrived haggard and unkempt. He described how the flames were sweeping through the city. Total destruction was in sight. Many other refugees soon poured into San Diego and Ocean Beach.

When Daddy's friend turned up, he had no luggage, only a large pair of scissors. I stared at the scissors and listened, fascinated, while he explained why he had brought them—and nothing else. As he threw on his clothes in the first panic, he saw those large paper-scissors on his table. He seized them and clung to them as though they were precious all through the earthquake. He didn't know why. He gave the scissors to mother as a souvenir. For years she treasured them; then they were lost.

We never saw the young man again but the consequences of that dreadful earthquake were disastrous for poor Daddy. Ocean Beach was in the earthquake zone. Nobody for a long time to come would buy land thereabouts. Poor 'Burkley Deeltry' once more lost his job and once more we faced ruin. Daddy had only saved a little money. Mother had yet again to prove herself the dauntless pioneer type. Her love for her husband was deathless—like her belief in him. She announced that she would set to work to try and earn money with her pen.

We packed up and left California.

I did not mind leaving Ocean Beach. A child gets used to being switched from house to house, and school to school, and, personally, I do not think it did me much harm, despite what modern psychiatrists have to say about 'need for security'. Possibly, though, it made me rather difficult and too much of a 'Know-all'—I was growing fast mentally and physically.

What flashes of remembrance can I summon up of those two years in California?

Eating wonderful oranges that tasted sweeter and more exquisite, picked fresh from the trees, than any fruit I have eaten since. In fact, after I left California, I spat out the first orange that was bought for me in New York. It tasted quite bad.

Going to that little day school near our bungalow each morning, carrying my picnic case in which sandwiches had been packed, and which I ate out in the sunshine at midday with the other children. Learning to roller-skate, and becoming quite adept.

Watching my step-father shoot a wild cat in order to put it out of its agony when it was being squeezed to death by a large snake which attacked it under our bungalow. I shall never forget that cat's appalling screech of agony before the merciful bullet silenced it for ever.

Seeing for the first and last time a whole bungalow being transported on wheels along our rough road. The family that

39

owned it were moving from one site to another. (No doubt this was the forerunner of our modern pre-fabs!)

Finding my first admirer—a little American boy, the same age as myself with snub nose and freckles—who told me that I was 'mighty purty'. When I proudly repeated this to my mother, she raised her brows and told me that I must not be conceited.

Then bidding goodbye to California, the golden land of oranges and of promises never fulfilled for the Dealtrys. I was never to see it again.

The next time I had the chance, twenty years later, was when I first started to become well known as a novelist. Hollywood invited me to go there and work on film-scripts. I refused. I would not leave my children for such a long stretch. And since then there has always been some reason why it has been impossible for me to return to America.

Gathering together their meagre savings, Mother and Daddy decided to go back to New York. We sailed on a cargoboat which was just due to leave San Francisco. We were to call at Panama, cross the Isthmus, by train, to Colon, then travel by another boat through the Caribbean on to New York. It was cheaper than the train. My adventure-loving mother and step-father also thought it would be a great experience.

Fortunately for me I remember quite a lot about that journey, especially my last glimpse of San Francisco. We went by tram to the docks. Just one single line ran through the ruined city. Poor 'Frisco, it looked much as some of the bombed cities in Europe must have done after an aerial attack. Most of the buildings were flat; so many of them in those days were built of wood; there were no strong super-structures or foundations such as we have today.

When they rebuilt San Francisco, they paid more attention to the possibilities of future earthquakes, but when we saw it in 1906 it was a terrible sight. It was grimly deserted. We were told that, among other things, the great Zoo of which the city was so proud had been destroyed. Many of the animals died in the fire. A few ferocious ones survived and roamed the wrecked city, and outskirts, terrifying the refugees who were harboured in hastily erected camps on the hills.

I remember it all.

During the voyage to Panama, mother happily coquetted not only with her husband but with all the ship's officers who adored the fascinating Australian. She had a wonderful time and as long as I was not too disobedient, I was left in peace to wander around as I wished.

I regret, of course, that I made that long interesting voyage at quite so young an age because I can imagine now how fascinating it must have been for the adults. I was the only child on board. I had no one to play with; however, I was occasionally allowed to fish with Daddy who tried to catch the elusive flying fish which are considered such a delicacy in the Pacific. They are difficult to land. The chief bait on board was cat-fish. I was allowed to angle for the cat-fish!

Those fish really do have heads that make them look like small silver cats with whiskers. I picked one up by the tail while it was still wriggling (against Daddy's warnings). The creature swung round in a semi-arc and bit me between two fingers—another little scar for me. The bite festered. A badly trained medical gentleman on the boat was so flustered that he plunged my small hand straight into over-strong carbolic. It took the skin off. My arm was in a sling for the rest of the voyage.

Now I became the centre of attention. Cries of pity and gifts of sweets came from the passengers. I really began to enjoy myself. What was more, the Captain discovered that I had a 'voice'. One evening my mother played charmingly, and her little daughter sang. It was quite a concert, with some of the crew and many of the passengers—mostly men—attending.

I can even remember the name of the song that was such a hit: *The Miller's Daughter*; a sad little ditty about a miller's daughter who was wooed by a fisherman who perished in the cruel, cruel sea; followed by the suicide of the miller's daughter. Apparently I delivered this with such drama that it drew a tear even from the eye of the hardened second mate

41

who gave me a dime and told my mother that I 'sure was cute'.

I think mother thought all this adulation bad for me but there was little more to come once we arrived at New York.

The Panama Canal was then in process of being built. We had to spend the night in Colon and sail on to New York next morning.

The night in Colon, at that time even less civilised than Panama, was unforgettable. The place was quite primitive—rather like those shanty towns you see, today, on 'Westerns'. We stayed at the one and only hotel—a sordid place filled with cut-throats, drunks, adventurers and labourers of all nationalities who were working on the Canal.

Nothing had ever been seen there before like my elegant mother or her husband. I—the little girl with her white skin and long chestnut hair—was stared at fiercely by half-breeds and rough-bearded men. This terrified my mother who believed that we would all be murdered in our beds.

Her terror increased when she found that our bedroom was alive with bugs. That to her was worse than death. Even then her Colonial courage did not fail. She sent Daddy down for some paraffin, put a few drops in four saucers and placed these under the feet of the iron bedstead in which·I was to sleep. She stripped off the sheets, threw them into a corner and spread her own rug for me to lie on. It was too hot for any covering—well over ninety degrees.

Dripping with perspiration, I lay in the bed, wide-awake, while my mother and step-father sat on either side of me on their hard wooden chairs. I enjoyed watching the bugs trying to escape from the paraffin.

We listened to the roars of drunken voices and the sound of a cracked piano coming up from below. Like this, we all three spent the night. Yawning and weary in the morning, we hastened with our luggage to the docks and boarded our respectable ship.

I'm a bit hazy about the rest of that voyage except that we called at various lovely little islands. But I do recall one terrible storm and being told by Mother and Daddy that after we left a certain island, it sank beneath the sea, never to rise again. This appealed enormously to my childish imagination. I often thought about that island buried under the Atlantic waves and all that must have gone down with it. It cannot be wondered at that after such experiences I grew up too rapidly. I was soon rather mature for my age, but mother stubbornly refused to recognise this. How irritating I must have been! Always in the way. Always, in some kind of trouble; imagining myself misunderstood *and*, I am sure, self-centred, which any lonely child is apt to become.

On board I made a habit of wandering down to the steerage which was full of poor South American families. They were fascinated by my white skin and bright hair. Unfortunately one stout Mexican lady kissed me on the cheek and left there a rash finally diagnosed as a *tropical fungus*. It looked like ringworm. The nasty moment arrived when the Health Authorities came aboard after our ship docked in New York harbour. They examined me and were suspicious of my skin condition and afraid that it might be highly infectious.

We were ordered to Ellis Island.

My mother really broke down then. Nothing my step-father could say comforted her. It was a disgrace to be detained on Ellis Island with the riff-raff of the immigrants and other detainees. The Dealtrys were put in a kind of enormous cage, there to be watched as though dangerous, or just curiosities.

My frantic mother then remembered a friend in New York with some influence to whom she could appeal for help. This man responded. He arrived next day and got us out of the ghastly detention camp.

Mother and Daddy were pretty shaken. To me it was just another experience—and quite entertaining.

Next morning, the Dealtry family re-entered New York City.

It is an interesting fact that the small hotel in which rooms had been reserved for us was totally destroyed by fire that very night and most of the guests died. So it turned out after all that my skin-trouble had possibly saved our lives.

Such is Fate.

43

8

MORE trouble awaited us.

Mother and Daddy rented a small apartment in a cheap part of the city. To be forced to live cheaply in New York was no fun. The apartment was tenement-class. Mother immediately tried to make some sort of home out of the ugly room and started to write again. She was a born home-maker. She managed to produce a few short stories which, to her delight, she sold to a popular magazine. She wrote with some talent and determination. Soon she began to earn regular money.

My first impression of an impecunious woman-author scribbling, late into the night was my mother in that New York apartment. She wrote every line by hand. (She had a beautiful rounded hand-writing full of character.) Daddy hired a cheap old machine and typed her manuscripts. What they wanted now was to get enough money together to buy our fares back to England.

America had failed this romantic couple. Berkeley Dealtry was too English—too 'public school', to endear himself to the tough middle-class Americans who were inclined to laugh at the 'laa-de-dah' English type. He knew he would never do any good out there. Mother was by now not at all well and apprehensive of the future.

In spite of her efforts it was soon obvious that there was small hope of her making enough to save more than a few dollars. She could barely pay the rent, or eat, on what she was earning. Too many manuscripts were returned.

Then Daddy was offered a job working on the Panama Canal. Not much of a job, but anything seemed better than nothing. He was ashamed because the financial burden was falling entirely on Mother and, anxious to play his part, he left her alone with me for the first time since their elopement and marriage.

The parting nearly killed Mother. I remember her crying miserably at nights. It couldn't have been much fun for her living with a difficult, high-spirited child of ten in a poor flat on the East Side. I could not have been a sympathetic companion for her. I was constantly trying her patience. I asked so many questions, she couldn't answer. I wanted so badly to spread my wings and make use of my vivid imagination. I was far too vital, and she was ill. She just couldn't tackle me.

I remember one quite amusing but typical episode.

I had annoyed her all day—I was disobedient and refused to keep quiet while she wrote. There was nobody to amuse me. I was naughty because I was so bored. Finally I was sent to bed. Mother told me she would come in and spank me with a slipper (a thing she had never done before). Alarmed at this prospect, I used my ingenuity, looked for and found the Bible which belonged to Daddy, and which was his, in fact, when at Clifton College where he was educated.

When my mother came in to administer the corporal punishment, she found me sitting up in bed, the big Bible on my knees. I was reading it, my face bearing a horribly smug, meek expression. Despite her anger, Mother broke down, laughed and cried and forgave my transgressions.

'Oh, Denise,' she said, '*do* try to be a good girl. You don't realise what I am going through!'

I didn't! What child of ten can understand or estimate the depths of grief and despair to which an adult may sink? Most children are concerned only with their own affairs.

There followed a grim time. Mother plodded on with her work not very successfully. Berkeley contracted yellow fever soon after he settled down in Panama. He went into hospital and wrote frantically to mother for help. He needed money. Mother telegraphed him all that she had and she and I went on meagre rations.

Afterwards, we learned that an American patient in the same ward as Daddy, and who was discharged before Daddy, robbed him. Daddy, too trusting, had asked the man to go to the post office on his behalf and collect the money Mother had cabled.

The wretch never came back. He bolted with the money she had earned and parted with at such a cost to herself—and me.

When Daddy complained, the hospital authorities shrugged their shoulders and said he should not have trusted the man.

With his health enfeebled, Berkeley finally returned to his job on the Canal. Only later did Mother learn that he had in fact been saved by a beautiful Spanish courtesan who fell in love with the handsome Englishman and allowed him to live in her flat. She financed him until he was on his feet again. Although he paid her back, it was scarcely an edifying episode. It was also the first of many infidelities. Daddy was not the faithful type. However, there was only one woman he ever *really* loved—that was my mother; of that I am sure.

Meanwhile poor Mother hit on what she genuinely believed to be an excellent scheme for me. Nothing, in fact, could have been more cruel.

She found out the name of that school in Flushing to which my father and Aunt Lilian had sent me while I was living with Uncle Charles.

Children are often oddly reticent about their troubles. I had never mentioned to Mother the name of the awful woman who ran that school, or of the brutalities practised upon me there. So Mother just thought how 'nice' it would be for me to go back to a place where I would be no stranger.

She telephoned the school and was told that the headmistress, my old enemy, was dead. Her husband still ran the place with the aid of his female staff. He seemed to have been a more kindly person than his wife for when he heard my mother's pitiful tale of being stranded in New York and of me, the niece of the great Charles Klein, being in such straits—he offered to take me in for what sum Mother could afford. Then, if things got better she would pay more. Like this it was arranged.

I remember the man coming to New York to fetch me. I did not recognise him. He did not know me, either. I had hardly ever seen him. He appears to have been away a great deal in the old days and had nothing much to do with the school. Mother kissed me goodbye. She believed that she could do more, and better work, once rid of me. She was hoping, too, that my step-father would soon return to her. She found his absence intolerable.

It was only during the train journey to the school that the scene began to become familiar, that there crowded into my mind the ugly memories of the past and how terribly unhappy I had been. I dissolved into tears and refused all comfort.

I never really felt safe or happy in the school although I cannot complain that I received the unkindness that was shown me before. The new teachers were quite nice to me; but the 'mix-up' in my mind grew worse. I couldn't understand anything. *Why* had everybody hated me and nearly beaten me to death in this school when I was six? *Why* had they told me then that my mother was dead, when, all the time, she was alive? Nobody answered those questions.

I began to have nightmares and to feel homesick even for our poor New York apartment and my impatient mother. It was home. Home counts to a child. That sickness of heart was not to leave me for many years. I was *always* homesick in the future when sent away.

Suddenly all payments from my mother ceased. The headmaster received frantic letters from her saying that she was ill and penniless. She begged him to keep me in school for one more term. She assured him that her husband was now on the way back from Panama and that she hoped soon to be able to send a cheque for my schooling.

But the 'head' had had enough, and regretted his original charity. Once again my trunk was packed. I was taken by a teacher to New York and left at Mother's flat—with apologies.

I received a mixed welcome. Mother by that time was overworked, over-worried, and really very ill with an internal complaint which had been growing worse ever since she left California.

There was nothing 'in the kitty'. My arrival was the signal for poor Mother's total collapse. Unconscious, half dying, she was removed that same night by ambulance to the City Hospital.

I sat in the middle of the shabby, deserted sitting-room— crying. I did not know what would happen to me now. Mother had pawned everything of value, including her few jewels. There was no money. I knew that—even at ten years old.

Into my life came Uncle Albert.

He was a bachelor, a 'rough diamond' who occupied the apartment above ours. He had fallen deeply and sincerely in love with my mother. There was no question of any love-affair. He knew well that her heart was in Panama, but thought the brave, beautiful Australian with the big eyes and charming smile was the most wonderful person he had ever met. When he learned that she had been taken away and had to have an immediate, major operation, he did what he thought the best thing for the deserted child. A convent must be found for her.

He made enquiries and discovered an establishment for poverty-stricken orphans run by a Roman Catholic religious order. There, I was taken by Uncle Albert who departed after kissing me (tears in his eyes), assuring me that he would visit me and my mother every day and that I would not have to stay there long.

For me it meant an extraordinary metamorphosis ... straight from a smart boarding school for the Daughters of Gentlemen to an orphanage! Believe me, that sort of establishment, in 1907, was no fun for little children. It largely resembled the grim sort of place described by Dickens.

The nuns were excellent women but over-strict. They had taken a vow of poverty. They had hundreds of orphans to look after. There could be no generosity or favouritism. Each child must rise or fall—it was a case of the survival of the fittest. They had no interest in my family tree!

The girls slept two in a single bed—head to foot. It was winter. We were always cold and nearly always hungry, too physically uncomfortable to appreciate lessons. There was no enforced education in those days so the teaching was negligible. For the most part, the children hung around in miserable groups trying, like Jane Eyre, to warm their frozen hands under their pinafores. We were constantly called to prayer.

I was desperately unhappy.

Mother knew nothing of this. I am sure if she had she would

48

have been horrified. Uncle Albert went to the hospital to see her and just told her that I was in safe hands with the holy sisters. She nearly died after her operation. When she came out of the hospital, I think she would have died if it hadn't been for the kindly Albert who organised her life for her and, himself, paid a 'daily' to cook for her and clean the apartment.

Christmas came.

My mother kept writing to me in loving terms, hoping that I was 'having a wonderful time at school'. The nuns censored my replies. No complaints of cold or hunger that I ever wrote reached her. I sent the happy letters dictated by the nuns.

Mother sent me a Christmas present—a doll for which she made the clothes.

After it came, I received a taste of the utter callousness and cruelty of small children towards each other.

I loved that doll. When I showed it off I was full of pride. One of the girls who was always ridiculing my English accent and manners discovered that the doll's dress had been sewn out of an old patched lace curtain. She showed it to the others. They began to laugh at my oddly dressed doll until I was convinced that my mother had sent me something degrading. I remember throwing the doll on the floor and crying until I was sick.

I did not tell Mother that story until I was grown up. I felt so sorry for *her*. She did her best at that time and her personal life must have been hell.

I don't really know what would have happened but for the kind and generous Uncle Albert. Incidentally, we none of us knew what became of him once we left the States but I salute his memory. He was a good man and an American citizen of whom the U.S.A. can well be proud. He did his best for the unlucky strangers from another land. He asked for no return.

As soon as Mother could walk again, she came to the convent to see me. She was stricken to see me looking thin and big-eyed. She realised for the first time the sort of Charity Institution poor Uncle Albert had innocently chosen for her child. She comforted me by telling me that she would soon fetch me and that we would all be travelling back to England.

Daddy wrote her desperate letters. He had recovered from the fever but felt ill and depressed and wanted to join her, but dared not leave his job—the only one he had. He begged Mother to go home and leave him in Panama until he had saved some money.

She decided to appeal to the only rich relative she had left —the man who had married her sister, Frances.

George Hutchinson by that time had become one of the best-known publishers in England.

My grandfather, George Cornwell, had died in 1905, aged eighty-nine—after marrying an Australian woman, younger than himself by twenty years (whom I later knew as 'Aunt Mary'). She was now living with Aunt Alice. Mother knew it was useless to ask either of *them* for money. But she hoped George would help.

I don't think he had really forgiven my mother for the scandal which reflected on his family after the Klein divorce. But persuaded by my gentle and kindly aunt, he relented sufficiently to cable mother the fare.

We boarded *The Philadelphia* and departed for London. My mother had no regrets. America had not been kind to her although I think she was anguished by the thought of leaving her husband so far behind. And I do truly believe that it was for my sake more than for her own that she left. Her sense of duty towards me was strong, yet when her emotions were involved, she was ruthless. Possibly my father and I were the only ones who ever really suffered from that hard side. Mother was sweet and kind to her close friends and adored by them.

Even on that voyage somebody fell in love with her—a wealthy manufacturer of shoes. He pursued her night and day. She strongly resisted his attentions.

It was fun for me.

He used to pay me sixpence to tie his deck-chair to my mother's in order that he should have the excuse to sit beside her. She would give me another sixpence to untie the chairs and carry his to the other side of the deck—before he appeared. I am ashamed to say that I took both sixpences and

50

acted for both parties. I have always been a good business woman!! Neither of them discovered my duplicity.

Now London received the exiles back again.

I think Mother was overjoyed to see the grimy, foggy old capital once more. But we were on the rocks financially.

Her sisters, Alice and Frances, were both fond of pretty, fascinating Clarice who was so much younger than themselves; but neither had approved of her leaving my father for a man who couldn't even support her. Secretly they admired her courage and loyalty, and Frances persuaded Uncle George to lend her yet more money in order to rent a small flat in West Kensington. I dimly remember this flat being on the ground floor somewhere in Queen's Club Gardens.

Mother was still far from well but, as she was forced to be the breadwinner again she set to work to find a regular English market for her stories.

9

MOTHER never wrote a selling novel but she had the gift of story telling. Since she left my father she had become philosophical and practical. She refused to be beaten. When told that what D. C. Thomson of Dundee wanted was a waif story in serial form, she somehow managed to produce it. Her first serial 'made' her and paved the way for our future. I think that story will be remembered even now by some of the very old readers up in Scotland. It appeared in the *Weekly Welcome* under the title of 'Little Meg'. The misfortunes of this poor waif from the slums—slums that no longer exist—made a terrific hit. Mother wrote her serial instalment by instalment, sending each one up to the editor in Dundee and waiting to have it approved. This was very often done by telegram. I can remember the delight with which she used to read those wires aloud—'*Instalment received excellent go ahead.*'

Sometimes a few chapters came back to be rewritten, a job

51

which my mother loathed (I've never liked it either!); but it had to be done. She proved unflagging in her efforts and undaunted by any failure.

I owe my knowledge of technique and the stubborn determination to 'get there' to her. So popular was the waif story 'Little Meg', that after she had written the required fourteen instalments readers began to send in appeals that it should not be allowed to finish. So the *Weekly Welcome* ran it for another ten weeks. Twenty-four instalments! I doubt if there has ever been a longer serial in any paper—every word written laboriously by Mother with her favourite fountain-pen.

Now she saw that she could make at least five or six pounds a week—a fortune in those days for us. She was paid at the rate of one guinea a thousand words, rising to two guineas a thousand after the successor to 'Little Meg'. Even at two guineas a thousand, it was hard work, but it meant that she could save a little and send the fare home to Daddy. Her heart was breaking for him.

I was then eleven—beginning to be what they call 'a little woman'. I was not tall but well developed for my age. One day outside our front door, Mother saw the milk-boy trying to kiss me. That settled things. She awoke to the awful realisation that sex was rearing its ugly head, and that I must be protected. Protection with her meant forbidding me ever to be alone with any boy, or man, and shutting her eyes to the fact that I was no longer the 'little innocent ignorant child' she wanted me to be.

On the day that Daddy arrived back in London, he and Mother were blissfully re-united.

I was sent to a cheap private school in Surrey which had been recommended. It was my mother's wish that I should be properly educated. I was in her estimation 'running wild'—becoming impossible to control.

There were still constant cries from her of:

'Oh, you are so like your father!'

I reached the stage of wishing passionately that Berkeley Dealtry had been my father, for then I felt sure my mother would have loved me more.

52

My next boarding school was not a success. The two elderly sisters who ran it needed the money but had little interest in the scholastic progress of their pupils. They were really interested in nothing but their four Persian cats. The pupils were badly fed and I think the old ladies must have taken a kind of sadistic pleasure in making the hungry pupils stand around in order to watch these pampered Persians being fed on large plates of salmon, and saucers of cream.

It was enough to make even an animal-lover resentful!

Mother found this out when I went home for the holidays. She had meant well but admitted that this school was a mistake. She took me away. I looked none too well and, as I was nothing if not frank, I finally confided in her the fact that I had received instructions in sex from 'one of the girls'. Unfortunately it was sex of a smutty variety and when Mother heard about it, she immediately decided that I must be sent to a convent again. I *needed* the holy nuns, she declared.

I protested but 'Fidelis', the London convent she eventually found, turned out to be a huge success—the nicest school of them all. The nuns were willing to take me for a moderate fee. and it was a fine place. I spent six happy years there—perhaps the happiest of my life—although this sort of remark is so often made with sarcasm.

'Fidelis'—which is still a flourishing girls school—is attached to the Roman Catholic church on Central Hill in Upper Norwood; a big grey building surrounded by trees. Now, alas, also surrounded by council houses. But when I was a child there were meadows and woods attached to our school grounds.

The nuns belonged, originally, to an order in Northern France—*La Vierge Fidèle*. They had come over to England in the days when Roman Catholic institutions were being closed down in France and settled in London. The teaching was extraordinarily good, if not up to modern standards. Certainly we learned to speak French. This was compulsory. The teaching nuns were erudite women from good families. It was a cosmopolitan atmosphere—the daughters of both rich and poor went there.

53

My uniform was bought. I can see myself plainly as I must have looked, a funny plump little figure in a black dress with the high white linen collar which we sewed on for ourselves, every Saturday, starched and clean. Indoors, we also put on typically continental black overalls, and we wore black shoes and thick woollen stockings.

The nuns had a unique form of 'Punishment and Reward'. Blue ribbons were pinned to our shoulders. On those ribbons the nuns would sew a silver stripe to mark one week's good conduct. Four of these silver stripes could be exchanged for a gold one. The more gold stripes you had, the better your report. It became a burning ambition with me to glitter with gold—like a senior naval officer!

There was an awful lot of praying but I flung myself fervently into the religious side of life. My knees grew hard and calloused. My mind teemed with visions of the saints. At every turn, through cloisters and class-rooms, one's gaze met lurid pictures of suffering Christs, meek Madonnas, and twisted, tortured martyrs. It all had a strong influence upon me; but not a bad one, for I needed *something* into which I could pour my surcharged sentimental heart. Why not give that heart to religion? I became devoted to the Roman Catholic Church but was never allowed to forsake the Protestant faith.

The holidays put paid to any hopes the good nuns had of gathering me into the fold. Mother believed in a convent education but not the faith. Daddy was an agnostic. The moment I got home my rosary was taken from me and my holy pictures torn up. This all added to the general confusion in my mind, for I still remembered my early Christian-Science training, and often in later years listened to theosophical arguments between Daddy and my brother Adrian when he visited us. Then, back I would go to the gleam of candles and odour of sanctity in my convent, and once again I would throw myself at the foot of the Cross.

I have a vivid picture of the visits we children paid, morning and night, to our church. In the dim light I would kneel and pray, or say my rosary, and feel all the difficulties of the day melting away like the wax that dripped from the tall candles on the altar.

The spicy odour of incense became to me as dear and familiar as any scent I have ever used. I learned to make the responses in Latin. I genuflected and crossed myself, saying '*Mea culpa*' and beating my breast with passionate fervour. I was caught up by the drama of the Mass and Benediction.

I was also taught to make what they called *Novenas*—nine days of constant prayer, of sacrificing something that I liked. Then one sad day (and now I must confess I am being cynical) my new found Deity failed me. I almost recanted.

I had received a letter from Mother saying that she could not afford to have me home for the holidays. (By then she had moved down to Cornwall and it was an expensive train journey.)

Much as I loved the convent it meant fairly harsh discipline and we were too much concerned, for such young children, with preparation for the life to come. I needed relaxation; and in my sentimental heart I adored my glamorous mother.

One of the nuns told me that if I made a *Novena* to Mary, Mother of God, She would take pity on me, and my mother would relent and send for me for the Easter break.

I prayed with terrific concentration.

On the ninth day of prayer and self-abnegation I rose from my knees filled with renewed hope.

The next morning I received a letter from Mother regretfully but firmly confirming the fact that I must remain at school for the Easter holiday.

It took me a long time to recover from that blow. Once again—like the child who had knelt in a cold lavatory praying to be saved from her thrashing—I felt that it was not much use praying.

I confided in one of the nuns. She found if difficult to win me back to my old faith or belief in prayer. But I have never been one to bear resentment and I didn't bear it for long against the seemingly heartless Mother of God who had ignored my *Novena*! I was soon cheerfully and optimistically going down on my knees to pray again.

Looking back, I bless the day when Mother sent me to 'Fidelis'. I made many friends there both among the religious community and the pupils.

10

I STILL visit one of the nuns. She is now over eighty. Her smiling face seems as fresh and young to me as it did fifty years ago, framed in the white wimple and black veil. The long years seem to roll back while we talk; and to her, the grey-haired grandmother is still 'little Denise'.

One need never really grow old!

Many things happened to me during those years at school. Life seemed to me for the first time to become regular and secure.

Of course the girls were very sequestered within those high convent walls. We were too strictly guarded from what the nuns rather timidly called 'the world'.

When we did emerge into the light of a normal secular existence we were positively scared, and as vulnerable as shorn lambs.

We knew nothing about men. We were taught that all things carnal were sinful. We were not even allowed to look upon our own naked bodies. For years I bathed in a kind of cotton bathgown, soaping myself demurely underneath it. Well do I remember the acute discomfort of this! The dear, silly nuns did not seem to realise that that was the very way in which to arouse curiosity. Enquiring young minds obviously begin to wonder what there is about a 'body' that could be so wicked!

We had only one mirror in the school—in our dormitory. Before this, we brushed our hair and plaited it. One night I wrapped myself in a sheet, toga-wise, and paraded in front of this mirror. The girls giggled. The nun who found me parading up and down like an actress was scandalised. I was given a lecture on modesty and told to pray God to cleanse me of this sinful interest in my appearance.

Mother once thought that she had done the right thing in posting me a religious postcard, a colourful reproduction of Raphael's *Madonna*. Before the Reverend Mother allowed me to have it, she inked a little pair of bathing drawers upon all the naked cherubs floating around the throne. In the good woman's mind, a young innocent girl must not be made aware of the physique of those male angels! How Daddy laughed when I showed him the bathing drawers. But even at home I was not informed why this had been done.

Such a training, is, of course, largely responsible for any young girl's curiosity. It is an amazement to me to remember how clean and wholesome we really were despite the stupidity of our parents and teachers.

World events hardly touched us in that convent school but I can recall the day when Mother St. Benedict, our headmistress, came and told us the terrible news that the *Titanic* had gone down. To us, this was a dramatic interlude. That night we knelt and prayed for the souls of the departed.

The only men with whom we ever came in contact were an Irish priest (our convent Confessor) and an ancient gardener.

For me, such an event as being taken to the dentist in Norwood was an excitement which made the pain of a tooth extraction worthwhile. It meant that I could talk to A MAN. To enter any shop was an innovation. But such outgoings were rare and in the holidays Mother still kept me under rigid control.

In this manner all my emotions were harnessed until I was seventeen.

I did only moderately well at lessons. Being so close to the Crystal Palace, the convent pupils were taken there for exams. I passed my 'Junior Oxford' (equivalent perhaps to G.C.E.) but nothing higher. I was useless at exams. I won a prize for singing during a Musical Festival in the Crystal Palace and, later, one for swimming in the Palace Baths. I was never able to cope with maths, science, geography or botany! I failed dismally in those subjects. I came to the top only in English, history and elocution. But at least I proved myself a journalist by starting the *School Magazine* which prospered and is still being printed. For this, I wrote innumerable stories, poems and essays.

I suffered various minor hardships in that convent. For instance, being roused at six a.m., having to break the ice in my water jug on those dark, bitterly cold winter mornings; and wash in it—and I can still hear the voice of the nun who tapped a sort of wooden knocker together in order to waken the pupils while she intoned the first prayer of the day:

'*Jesus, Mary and Joseph!*'

Our drowsy young voices, still drugged with sleep, answered:

'*Pray for us!*'

I never really got used to the cold, waking in the dark, or going to church so early. There was no coddling for us. No stimulating games. We played lady-like basket ball and, even worse, tennis on a damp asphalt playground which was either full of rain puddles in the summer or slippery with ice in winter. Every afternoon, with a nun in charge, we walked in a long crocodile down Central Hill as far as Streatham Common and back to school again—our hands and feet frozen.

Inside the convent, however, there was generally a pleasant atmosphere. I grew fond of it—of the shining polished wood floors, the light airy classrooms, and the big 'hall' where we gathered for concerts or our school plays.

I have a vivid memory of the long row of tiny piano 'cells', only big enough for the instrument and stool. In one of these we had to practise immediately after morning Mass: before we were given even a hot drink or bite of food. Hungry and cold, I remember struggling to play: chipped keys—broken pedals—awful tone. Yet my love of music triumphed and I even looked forward to those harsh half hours of rigorous practice on an empty stomach!

I also remember a glorious moment of school life when—in my last year—I won the Good Conduct Prize. I was amazed. I had been voted for by the mistresses and pupils themselves. I felt rather smug.

58

I treasure a picture of myself on Prize Day, wearing a long white dress, an expression of self-conscious piety on my hot pink face, stepping on to the platform where the Bishop of Southwark handed me a book and placed a crown of lilies on my head.

I thanked his lordship. I curtsied to the Mother Superior. I tried to catch the eye of a nun whom I adored—in vain. She flatly refused to return my devotion. As I came down to join the other girls, I noticed them all stifling their laughter. I was highly incensed. Why should they laugh because I had received the distinguished crown? I was to get the answer to that question when I saw myself in the dormitory mirror later. The Bishop had accidentally placed the lilies at a drunken angle over one side of my brow. I couldn't have looked sillier!

The other day I found a faded photograph of a painting of myself in a long robe, wearing a blue mantle, and another crown—the copy of the crown worn by St. Elizabeth of Hungary. I played this part in a school play, at the age of sixteen. An artist-friend used to paint our scenery. The senior girls made all the costumes under the supervision of a wonderful nun whom we called Mother St. Anselm. She had an amazing sense of the dramatic, and produced our plays quite professionally. It was a time when the whole religious community relaxed. We were really allowed to throw our hearts into our dramatic productions.

I have an amusing memory of myself with my equally dramatic school-friend, Naomi Nightingale (now Lady Boynton) playing parts in a highly religious piece which included a scene in which we were burned at the stake. My co-martyr, Naomi and I, established a friendship which still flourishes.

My screams were so terrible that the Reverend Mother sent a note up to the stage. It said:

'*There is no need for Denise to be quite so realistic. It is too distressing for the audience.*'

I felt indignant that I must muffle the yells of agony which I was sure were correct.

My reports while I was at the convent were nearly always satisfactory. This amazed my mother who could not understand why the nuns found me so tractable. I just seemed to fit in with the life there, but my life at home during the holidays continued to be tempestuous.

At the beginning of my convent education, Mother left the flat in West Kensington and rented a pretty little Victorian cottage, with a garden, in Fox Hill, not far from the Crystal Palace.

I first went to 'Fidelis' as a day scholar, but Mother did not enjoy having me at home, so I soon lived in as a boarder. Mother was still frantically absorbed in her husband and she could not write in peace, she said, with me in the house. I disturbed her.

While I was still a day girl I made friends with Kenneth and Ethel Lodge and their son Toby, who lived in a big house opposite our cottage. One day I was allowed to buy a white rat. It became my constant companion. Mother shuddered but let me keep the little rat because I was so crazy to have a pet of my own. I adored that little white creature with its twitching nose and red eyes.

Mother bought a piano and sang sentimental ballads every night to her husband. Mother wrote love stories. Mother talked of nothing but love. Quite understandably I too longed for love, and for the day when I would be loved in return.

The Lodges soon adopted me as their niece, and became as dear and close as any real relatives could be. They brought me great happiness. Kenneth Lodge was a stockbroker. He painted portraits for a hobby. I used to sit for him.

They were both good to me. I had many gay tea-parties in their house. It was a friendship that was to last until the dear old Lodges were laid to rest in their respective graves.

Uncle Kenneth died on that same night that the Crystal Palace blazed to the high heavens, and all that miraculous glass was shattered for ever. Aunt Ethel followed a few years latter.

Toby drifted out of my life but re-entered it a short time ago when he sent me the exquisitely painted portrait of Aunt Ethel's mother—whom I called Great-Aunt Sophia. It is one of the finest works by the English artist R. A. Buckner. He painted it in Rome a hundred and twenty years ago. Now Great-Aunt Sophia graces my drawing-room. She is of exceptional beauty and holds a little King Charles spaniel in her arms. The painting reminds me of the happy hours I spent as a schoolgirl in the Lodges' dining-room, eating crumpets for tea and looking up at Aunt Sophia's wonderful face. In that house with those kindly people, I tasted at last the joys of normal family life. Mother remained fundamentally anti-social—she never entertained my friends nor would she go and see them. She wanted only to be alone with Daddy. She maintained that once she started to know people, she would be caught up on the social web and find less time for her writing. Nowadays, I see her point of view somewhat, although I am much more gregarious. I love people and parties.

In my school holidays I liked to type my mother's manuscripts, which she often let me do. It was good training for me. I could type fast, with two fingers, before I was twelve.

11

JUST before my thirteenth birthday Mother considered that it was time I saw my two brothers. The Kleins were now living in London. Mother wrote to my father through the solicitors. The two boys were detailed to take me out from school although father disliked the idea of their making contact with me.

I shall never forget my first sight of them. I had not seen them since they were little boys. I scarcely recognised them. Adrian was tall and serious with light brown hair, large blue eyes and a big curly mouth. He looked what he was—an artist. Daryl was shorter, and very shy. It was Adrian who did all the talking. He had a brilliant mind which was to bear fruit at a later date when his paintings and knowledge of advanced photography made him famous.

The boys—very American still in dress and accent—took

me to the Crystal Palace to see 'The Bioscope'; the forerunner of modern films. It was a shaky, jerky little affair, calculated to ruin the eyesight, but it seemed to me (to use one of Adrian's sayings) an *extraordinary phenomenon.*

During tea we talked, but not of the past. Young people are more interested in the future. Adrian decided that I had learned too much 'sloppy sentimentality' from my mother and must be taught to appreciate higher forms of art, literature and music. He delivered one of his many lectures on the glories of Bach and Beethoven, gave me my first volume of Keats, and instructed me in the Impressionist works by Turner who was then his god.

After that day, I was not to see Daryl again for a long time.

He was a strange, silent boy who later became a writer of serious novels and also proved himself no mean poet.

His first job was with the Dunlop Rubber Company in Singapore. Later he went on to China where he lived for many years. Shanghai was then still a great international city. And to use his own words *'My job brought the contact, the means of cultivating a devoted self-assignment with Chinese conditions which endures to this day.'*

In 1919 Daryl published a book entitled *With The Chinks* —a story of the Chinese Labour Corps in which he served during the 1914–18 war.

His present hobby lies in buying and restoring beautiful old houses. In this he is aided by his wife, Ivy, who composed the music for a song which was published in time for the Coronation and accepted by the Queen; but my mind has leapt too far ahead. I must return to my schooldays.

When I was fourteen, Mother moved from Norwood and went down to Newquay. She and Daddy rented *'Skerryvore'*, a pleasant modern house on the edge of the cliffs. During the winter storms it was shaken by the thunder of the gigantic waves as they boomed and beat against the rocks below.

Mother liked this place and enjoyed the storms. I used to lie awake in bed listening to the howl of the wind. Storms still make me, as they did then, feel sad and nervous. The Cornish gales had such an effect on me that I eventually wrote a morbid poem on the subject. I was at the time aged about fifteen.

> *I would the sea were quieter,*
> *For at night I cannot sleep*
> *The waves kept moaning, sobbing*
> *Till I feel that I must weep.*
> *I lie here in the darkness,*
> *And my eyelids burn and smart.*
> *For the sea's perpetual crying,*
> *Seems to break my very heart.*
> *Oh, relentless waves, be silent,*
> *Let me rest my aching head.*
> *You are filling me with madness,*
> *And I wish that I were dead!*

Morbid and theatrical for one so young but during my next three years in 'Skerryvore' I was not altogether happy. There was perhaps a little more life for me in Newquay. I found one friend down there to play with me and I usually returned from the convent for my holidays longing for Mother and my own home again.

At this time the man destined to become Mother's third husband arrived on the scene; Sydney Groom, B.A. He had scholarshipped from a Grammar School in Norwich to Sidney Sussex College, Cambridge. He had just taken a post as maths master in a Newquay boys' school. He was a pale, good looking young man with mild blue eyes, a shy smile, and a stubborn chin. He got on well with Daddy who had a great sense of humour and was friendly with most people. Sydney also fell head-over-heels in love with my fascinating mother.

Mother was then forty-two. She had put on a lot of weight but was still a lovely woman. It soon became apparent to, but by no means resented by, Daddy that Sydney adored her. It amused him, I think. He was never jealous.

Once again I felt out of it all, so I turned in earnest to

writing poetry. It became a sort of outlet for my emotions. Unhappiness often produces the best work. Today I am amazed by the fact that I was barely sixteen when I wrote the following verses. I could not have written them today.

> *A child alone in the utter darkness*
> *Suffers the pain of death;*
> *Gropes with his tiny fingers. white with fear,*
> *Waits for the ghostly shadows to appear.*
> *Listens to eerie voices in his ear*
> *While he holds his sobbing breath.*
> *A gleam of light is a welcome innovation,*
> *Free the baby soul from its desolation.*

> *Am I then still but a nervous weakling,*
> *I who have lived long years?*
> *For at times my soul is wrapped in a nervous dread*
> *My heart in the isolation of the dead,*
> *With blinding, aching madness in my head*
> *Filled with unreasoning fears.*
> *Oh, God. it isn't the darkness ... that I bless*
> *It's the sudden stab of mental loneliness.*

> *The inward fires I have long since crushed*
> *Tauntingly smoulder yet.*
> *I am tired, perhaps, and I long for evasive sleep.*
> *I am tired, and the hills to climb are bitter-steep*
> *Without a hand to clasp or a love to keep.*
> *My heart, do I then forget,*
> *E'en in the midst of the loneliness I've hated,*
> *God must be with the soul He has created.*

In the over-heated sentimental atmosphere created in the home by Mother, it is not surprising that I, myself, became too sentimental. I remember, one evening, sitting beside her and asking her why she didn't hold *my* hand instead of my stepfather's. She looked at me coldly with those fabulous eyes of hers and said:

'You cannot *make* people love you, Denise. The sooner you learn this, the better.'

How right she was! But it was a lesson I had to assimilate gradually. Only after much pain and frustration did I master myself. Then I started to be more sensible and critical of myself. I learned patience, too. I told myself that one day I would most certainly find the right person to love and who would love me.

One day my brother, Adrian, reappeared; he came down to Cornwall bearded and long haired, wearing a marvellous black cloak. He was then only twenty, and right out of sympathy with Hélène and Father; in fact he joined with Mother in a mutual-dislike campaign against Father. This, of course, greatly endeared him to Mother!

She received him on his first visit as ardently as though he were a lover. She was glowing like a young girl. For this was Adrian, her first-born who she loved the best of her three children.

I, too, adored him and he made friends with my step-father whose excellent brain could keep up with his conversation which was usually on a high intellectual level. Nobody mentioned Father's name any more.

Adrian at this time had fallen in love with a girl named Angela. She was petite, dark-haired, intelligent and a clever violinist, youngest of the three daughters of Admiral Brackenbury.

She came down to Cornwall to see us and we were all fairly sure that this was the girl Adrian would one day marry.

12

I DEVELOPED a not unnatural desire to see my father—always positive that he would love me—I persisted in this until I wore Mother down and at last she wrote to Father, through the solicitors, stating that I had expressed this wish and that it was now up to him to decide whether or not he wished to gratify it.

To my surprise and delight, he invited me to visit him at his home 40 Avenue Road, St. John's Wood.

It was a great concession on my mother's part allowing this. I was crazily anxious to see this father whom I was supposed to resemble so strongly and whose affection and attention I had been so long denied.

The man who I called 'Daddy' took me up to London to see my father. He left me at the house.

I was shown into my father's studio. I saw a short dapper man with a mass of white hair, pink cheeks and a white moustache with little curled-up ends, sitting in front of a fire.

He rose as I entered. We looked at each other. I had meant to be dramatic and fling myself into his arms but an unusual shyness prevented me from doing so. I could see that he was embarrassed, too—no doubt feeling rather guilty about me. (Wife No. 3, Hélène, did not put in an appearance.)

He kissed me on both cheeks. Then we sat together on the sofa and talked. He asked me a few questions about myself but made no reference to my mother or her present husband. He seemed more interested in my musical education, also in telling me about his personal triumphs in the music world. I sat there staring into hazel eyes which were exactly the colour of my own, listened to his charming voice, and watched the way he moved his rather beautiful hands. Dumbly, I adored him. Rightly or wrongly, I was convinced that he was marvellous, and that I had missed the whole world by not being allowed to live with him instead of with an unsympathetic mother.

Only once did Father mention my mother's name and that was when I forced him into it by asking him if he remembered her. Then he frowned and answered:

'Yes, naturally. But I do not want to speak of her. Of course I realise she was only a baby when I married her. I should have known it would never work.' He refused to say more.

Then something rather sad and comic happened. Longing to impress him, I told him I could sing. At this, his eyes lit up. He told me to stand on the dais which he used for his pupils. He ordered, rather than invited me to sing for him. He was all enthusiasm now. Probably he thought that his own daughter might be a potential *prima donna*. At last, I felt real interest awakening in him; a real warmth between us. I was both blissful—and afraid.

He found a song which I knew. I rarely felt nervous, but by that time I began to be terrified, and to wish I had never started this. However, locking my hands behind my back, I sang the song to the best of my ability.

My voice sounded all too small to me in that famous studio that afternoon.

The *maestro* stopped playing. He looked up at me solemnly, then put away the music. He said:

'You must never sing again, Denise. Never! You have no talent at all. Absolutely none.'

I stepped off the dais, swallowing my bitter disillusionment. Tea was brought in. I ate my bread and butter and cake, half choking. My father never referred to my voice. I could see that I was counted 'out' by the great professor of singing. Right out! I was beginning to feel that I was a failure with my own father just as I had always been with Mother. The whole afternoon was a crushing disappointment.

Father seemed quite unaware of my distress. He took me in the garden and cut some roses from his special tree. He was fond of gardening, and there were still a few blooms on the bushes this October afternoon. He was very pleasant; finally he kissed me goodbye, patted my head and told me to be good, and that he would ask me to tea again one day soon.

He never did.

He sent me away with an autographed copy of his book *Musicians and Mummers*, his photograph and the flowers. When my step-father met me, he eyed the book and the bouquet gloomily but asked no questions about my father. We returned by underground to my aunt's house in Earl's Court where we were staying the night.

I was near to tears. I smelled the roses and tried to comfort myself that *he* had picked them for me and that he *did* love me but had been too overcome to show it. I was determined to be loved!

We were standing on the platform; a train rushed in. Suddenly my step-father seized the roses and flung them down on the line. Aghast, I watched the wheels crush them out of recognition. I turned on him.

'I hate you! Those were my father's roses. He picked them for me! I wanted to show them to Mother.'

'I shall buy you a better bunch,' he said emotionally. 'I will not have that man's flowers under the same roof as your mother.'

It all seems so dramatic and stupid now!

13

As I grew older my school holidays in Cornwall appeared to become awkward for Mother. I was no easy girl to manage, always on the defensive, struggling to assert myself. The subject of sex began to interest me a lot more. With Mother's frequent exhibitions of her passion for Daddy—they so often sat holding hands or kissing, or locking themselves in their bedroom—I could scarcely fail to ponder upon what went on behind that door, and what all this passionate love was about!

But Mother, living herself in a world of love-songs, tears and sighs, offered no explanations or alternative excitement to interest me. No parties, no theatres, no dances. None of the recreation provided in most homes for young people in the year 1913.

I was bored thoughout the holidays.

Suddenly I had a letter from Sibyl, my half-sister. She had settled in Paris, having divorced her husband, and left America. She had been living in France during all these years with Harry, her son, and her daughter, Ruth. (Harry was one of twins. The other had died at birth.) So nobody had seen Sibyl but now she came to England, and out of curiosity, called on my mother. But *that* wasn't a success.

Sibyl was a smart, elegant woman of the world. She and Mother had nothing in common. As for me, when she met me again she must have felt a sense of guilt because of her heartless treatment of me in the past.

She avoided future meetings. Many years were to go by, and I, myself, was a wife and a mother by the time I saw her again.

I was disappointed when Sibyl proved little more than a stranger. I needed so badly some wonderful being to whom I could attach myself and find some kind of affinity.

I became deeply fond of a young nun at my convent. I thought her holy and beautiful. I used to hang around, waiting to curtsey or open a door for her, missing various recreations just in order to see her pass by. I wept with intense grief because she received my devotion with icy indifference. When I loved, it could never be reasonably. It must always be a cyclonic affair. In time, like a cyclone, it became devastating. No wonder my poor mother found the task of bringing me up rather beyond her powers.

I stayed at the convent until I was nearly seventeen. Mother gave me a special party to celebrate that birthday; just herself, Daddy, and me, for dinner.

It was a sad and cruel day to remember. It should have been such a happy one. At last I was to 'put up my hair'. For the occasion, Mother had (perhaps misguidedly) bought my first evening dress for me. White charmeuse, with a low neck, and no sleeves.

I ran downstairs, conscious that I looked suddenly grown-up and rather nice; my chestnut hair pinned high on my head and my shoulders exposed for the first time.

'I say!' my step-father exclaimed, looking at me. 'You are quite lovely, Denise!'

Mother intercepted the look. There was an instant's silence; then she ordered me to follow her upstairs, found a large scarf and covered my neck and the curve of my girlish bosom.

The birthday party was continued in frozen silence. What Mother had read into Daddy's look, I did not know. Understanding came only at a later date. Then I pitied her. It must be terrible to feel such an agonising jealousy.

For the first time there followed misunderstandings and rows between mother and her husband, for which I was blamed.

Mother saw danger in keeping her seventeen-year-old daughter and attractive young husband together in the same house. It was not for this that she had sacrificed her time, her long hours of writing in order to pay for the home, and my school-bills. She seemed suddenly to hate me openly. She told me that she had lived to regret that my father had ever sent me back to her from America.

I was stunned and bewildered. Gradually I understood what she meant.

Then Daddy and I began to eye each other warily, and even in stony silence. It was the end of an old pleasant innocent association. We did not meet again except for meals. Night after night I shed wild tears. There seemed nothing left for me at Porth Bean. First I wanted to kill myself, then I toyed with the idea of going back to my convent and taking the veil. As for romance—I almost wondered if it existed or was a figment of my imagination. Reality was so grim, I could not endure to face it.

14

IT was perhaps a timely intervention when the famous newspaper proprietor, D. C. Thomson, from Dundee, and his wife arrived in Porth for a holiday. He came also to visit the most highly paid of his contributors—my mother.

Now everybody in Porth Bean had to 'put on a face'.

With the resilience and optimism of youth, I cheered up. Mother and Daddy seemed to forget their differences. The atmosphere became ordinary and friendly again.

The Thomsons came in the first motor car I had ever seen. One of those high old Daimlers with highly-polished brass lamps which are now to be seen in Old Veteran's Races on the Brighton Road.

Mr. Thomson and his wife took me for my first ride. I had only so far travelled by horse-omnibus in London, or one of the Newquay pony carts which they called 'jingles'; so to me the ride in that car was as fast and breathtaking as any Monte Carlo Rally.

Mother firmly refused to enter the demon chariot. From that time onward she developed a strange complex that would not allow her to drive in any car unless it was absolutely essential. She was highly nervous. Crossing roads in traffic terrified her, too. Sudden sharp noises made her go quite white, and tremble. At the first roar of thunder she would draw all the curtains in the house, shut the doors and sit in the hall where there were no windows, and she could not see the lightning.

She was like that until she died.

To this day, during a storm, I think what a good thing it is that my poor mother isn't alive to suffer through it. Yet she adored the tempests that swept the Cornish coast and the mountainous seas. She was really happiest when on the sea, and would, she said, have liked to have lived the remainder of her life on board ship, going round and round the world.

It was exactly the right time for David Thomson to meet me. He saw in me a potential author for 'Dundee'.

He stayed in Newquay not only two days as anticipated, for his wife developed typhoid fever, and it was two months before she could make the journey back to Scotland. They rented a furnished house in Porth. I remember the awe with which the great D.C. was regarded because he kept the telephone wires between Newquay and his Dundee offices open for hours on end. He must, they said in Porth, be a millionaire.

Mrs. Thomson recovered. By that time I had made my mark with the great D.C. He told Mother she could send me up to Dundee as soon as she wished, and that he would give me a job on one of his magazines.

I had been sent up to D. C. Thomson to be trained in journalism and I enjoyed my training, despite my loneliness. I owe a great deal to the Thomsons. I found little romance, however. Nobody took much notice of me. I had no money to spend. I slaved for a salary of £1 a week—gave seventeen shillings and sixpence a week of this to the old Scots lady, Miss Dow, with whom I lodged; and relied on Mother for a few shillings towards other expenses.

The evenings were deadly. Miss Dow had orders from my mother never to allow me to go out unchaperoned. I was still to be disciplined—obedient to rule.

How well I remember my first job on the paper; I was given an old badly-written manuscript which had, at some time, been bought by Thomsons, and told to reshape the story and make it fit for publication. They printed my final efforts and then I really began to feel that I was getting somewhere.

Life had its thrills. I went up to Dundee in the winter. A Christmas play was always performed annually by members of the office staff. Being a newcomer, nobody dreamed of offering me a part. Enviously I used to creep to the rehearsals, listen and watch, and wish I were the girl who played lead as an artist's model. It was a dramatic affair.

Two days before the performance was due to take place this girl developed a temperature and flu. Panic! There was no understudy! The producer tore his hair. He gathered the company together—myself, as usual, on the fringe, watching.

'What can we do? We're absolutely ruined!' he groaned.

I stepped forward. My cheeks were flaming red, but I had never been shy. I said:

'Please let me try the part.'

Everybody stared. My cheeks grew redder. They must all have thought that I had colossal cheek, and so I had. The producer stared. Somebody told him my name.

'You couldn't possibly learn the part in time,' he said.

'But I *know* it,' I said. 'I've been to all the rehearsals and I *know* the whole part of the artist's model.'

Silence. I don't think my heart has ever beaten so fast. Then he said:

'All right, let's hear you do it.'

At the end of the play, I also heard the intoxicating sound of applause. I had never enjoyed myself more. How I wished

Mother had allowed me to go on the stage! I was sure the world had lost a second Sarah Bernhardt. (I wonder how many thousands of young would-be actresses imagine the same thing!)

Anyhow *The Artist's Model* was a huge success. With joy and pride I sent home the cuttings of the reviews which appeared in the *Dundee Courier*; we played to the public for three nights.

Mother was pleased, but assured me I would be well advised not to abandon my writing career for the stage.

I might have stayed on in Dundee, only a serious outbreak of scarlet fever there decided my mother that I must go home. Not that she wanted me! She found life with Daddy more peaceful without me. But she gave me a welcome. Nobody seemed to want to carry on past differences, and I, personally, did not bear malice. No matter how wretched I was when I left Cornwall, I rushed back there again eager to be reunited with my mother.

It was only eight months before the dark menace of the First World War became more than a mere threat, and the terrible storm was to break with full force over Europe.

August 4th, 1914. The Germans marched into Belgium. In Newquay, in the main streets, megaphones gave out the news that England was at war with Germany.

From that day onward there was to be great change in my life as well as in the lives of millions of other people. It was goodbye for ever to the old peaceful existence and to the splendours—and miseries—of the early 1900s.

Daddy, having been a regular officer, was on the Reserve. Uncle Cosmo, too, was recalled. They were immediately detailed to help train the men of Kitchener's Army.

Porth Bean was hurriedly sheeted, shuttered and closed down. My mother, terror stricken that she might lose her adored one, followed Daddy who was with the Suffolks. Later they went to Shoreham-by-Sea. There, as a captain, Daddy joined the 9th East Surrey Regiment.

I was not to be allowed to go with Mother. She sent me to Brighton to live with my old aunt, Mrs. Robinson, who was now running a guest-house in Kemp Town. In this not very inspiring work she was helped by old Mrs. Cornwell (known as Aunt Mary), who was once married to my grandfather.

It was yet another move for me.

I found wartime Brighton a hive of activity. Already the Pavilion was being turned into a hospital. Other smaller Red Cross hospitals were springing up all over the town. We were plunged into a regime hitherto undreamed of. Blackout curtains were drawn across the windows because of Zeppelin raids at night. We became familiar with rationing, and soon scarcely a man in 'civvies' was to be seen.

It was khaki, khaki, soldiers everywhere. Railway stations were the scene of tearful farewells or frenzied reunions. The shadow of war and death hung over us. Hastily trained men were rushed to the front.

I attended First Aid classes and qualified as a V.A.D. nurse.

I flung myself enthusiastically into knitting, packing parcels for prisoners, and visiting the wounded. I met many officers who were attracted to me but by the end of the first year of war I had still not lost my heart.

I quite enjoyed living in Aunt Alice's Brighton home. It was always full of people and she was a most interesting old lady. Astrology was her passion. She spent her leisure hours casting horoscopes. She cast mine and everything she prophesied has come to pass—she was uncannily right. Her son, Sydney Carroll, came often to the house. He was a vital, arresting personality—soon to make his mark in theatrical enterprise and Fleet Street.

I had my first love affair.

One evening, a Canadian Officer whose name, I regret to say, I have forgotten, came to supper and afterwards alone with me he told me that he loved me. He removed the pins from my hair. That in 1914 was rather bold! I didn't really care for the quality of his kisses but hoped that I would in time learn to appreciate this passion. Suddenly my aunt came in, realised the situation, and suggested that the Canadian Officer should take himself home. Dear old auntie then gave me a lecture on sex and how a young girl should behave. This was

74

very enlightening. I didn't see the Canadian Officer again, but I decided that it might be better to find the right man in the future to unpin my hair!

From this time onwards, I think it might be said that I started on the Pursuit of Romantic Love which was to last a long, long time. Unfortunately what I found for the most part during this hopeless search was just passion. I had to learn that many men want to go to bed with a pretty girl—not waste time on romantic dalliance. It was a bitter pill for me to swallow—though I was forced to swallow it. The result was acute mental indigestion!

After a few months in Brighton—I was then eighteen and a half—Mother allowed me to join her and her husband in Shoreham.

I think she had begun to feel that she ought to let me live with her again. She had also gauged from my letters that I was becoming too interested in the opposite sex, and she didn't trust Aunt Alice—her too-tolerant elder sister—to discipline me rigorously enough. She decided to take control again.

Once in the little house which they had taken at Shoreham, I don't doubt Mother regretted once more opening the doors to me. She thought me too pretty. Daddy brought home many of the young officers of his Company—and there was trouble.

The subalterns with half an eye on me, and half on their Company Commander, flirted madly with me. I was responsive; Mother tried to restrain me.

'You *mustn't* be such a flirt, Denise!' she would protest.

I had stopped writing for the moment but Mother was still working—although now, of course, Daddy as an Army Captain with allowances was better able to support her.

I began to long for the day when I could be financially independent of them both.

Then I met an extraordinarily handsome young captain who was in Daddy's battalion. He seemed the answer to my prayers. He was clever, an Oxford Rowing Blue and he attracted me physically. We became very attached but he considered me too young to be married or even engaged. He believed that we should wait for the end of the war, anyhow,

75

before taking any irrevocable steps.

I loved him—with all the fervour of my young heart—but my joy was to be short-lived.

On the 9th August, 1915, the East Surreys moved from Shoreham to Blackdown Camp, Camberley. Before we knew where we were, the dark day that Mother dreaded arrived. The Brigade was ordered to the front.

Daddy and the other young officers with whom I had danced and flirted, marched out of Camberley and crossed the Channel to France.

Mother and I returned to our house in Shoreham.

For her it was a truly terrible time. Not only did she feel that she would never see her husband again, but she fell gravely ill and had to be removed to a nursing home in Lancing, there to have an emergency major operation.

She was lucky that the young man who operated on her— Barnard Sangster-Simmonds—was a brilliant surgeon in the making. Mother was, in fact, one of the first big private cases. (Later he became a famous gynaecologist and Senior Surgeon at the West London Hospital, Hammersmith.)

One week after her operation, the sword of Damocles that had been hanging so grimly over Mother's head, fell.

It was the 15th September, 1915, the day of that terrible battle of Loos; a battle that was fought desperately but lost.

Very few officers or men came out of the engagement alive.

At the nursing home where my mother lay so gravely ill, a telegram arrived and destroyed her life's happiness.

We regret to inform you that Captain H. A. B. Dealtry of the 9th East Surrey Regiment is reported wounded and missing.

It is a strange thing that my mother, who never thought herself psychic, knew that this was coming, for when I went to the nursing home to take her that telegram, dreading the news I had to break, she looked at me and said: 'Denise, I know why you have come. Daddy is dead. A few moments ago I heard the Last Post but nurse tells me there is no camp anywhere near this Home. It must have been just a terrible presentiment.' (Which, indeed, it was.)

A similar telegram was sent to the parents of the young Captain who had been so dear to me. He fortunately was later reported alive and well, and in a German prison camp. Daddy never returned. It is thought that he was blown to pieces while leading his men over the top.

Mother nearly died of shock and grief. It was too much even for a woman of her courage, but that obstinate streak which never accepted defeat eventually returned. She pulled through after a slow, agonising convalescence.

15

IN due course we returned to Cornwall and opened up our old home.

For me it was a privilege I had never before enjoyed to become the one upon whom Mother now leaned. In those dark days we grew much closer to each other. I felt that my devotion was at last returned, although I was sad that it was she who had to pay such a bitter price for this.

While she recovered from her operation we were more like sisters than mother and daughter. In her grief she was gentle and sympathetic towards me and I tried to comfort her for I knew it must have been a grim home-coming for her. Porth Bean was empty and sad. The laughter, the love, the music that she used to share with Daddy were missing.

For a long time she tried to believe that there was a chance he, like some of the others, might be a prisoner. There followed that long-drawn-out agony of trying to trace a missing soldier. We sent Daddy's photograph and a full description of him to every hospital, every Red Cross unit or prisoners' camp throughout Europe, France, Belgium, Holland, Italy and Germany; we left nothing undone.

It was terrible to watch Mother poring over the collection of small photographs which one received from the Commandants of these camps and hospitals. They were all likenesses of officers and men who had forgotten their own names, lost their memory, or been so injured that their identity was difficult to trace.

Poor Mother! Her big blue eyes would widen with hope then fill with tears again.

'I shall never see him again,' she said those words to me one morning.

Then she gave up hope. She began to live on her memories. But I received regular letters from my young Captain who was locked away in his *Kriesgefangenenlager*. I wrote to him regularly and sent him parcels. I heard from him in return and we kept this up for two years, then our interest in each other seemed to fade out and I never saw him again.

Mother disposed of the lease of Porth Bean. We sold most of the things and removed ourselves and a few treasures to Brighton. The old life was over. Mother thought it best to go to a place where we knew somebody. Aunt Alice was growing old and she lived then quietly with Aunt Mary in a flat in Brighton.

It was a sad world, and a bad war for Mother and Aunt Alice. Neither of them saw much of the other luckier sister, Frances (Lady Hutchinson). Her husband was a distinguished, successful man. They lived in luxury in a beautiful house in Sussex. But even their home was not left untouched by the tragic finger of war. The eldest girl, my cousin Dossie, had married a charming man named Guy Oliver, a captain in the Regular Army. He was killed only a few days before Dossie was due to join him for his leave in Paris. She was left to face life as a young widow with a baby son, Edward. She never married again, although she had many opportunities, for she was a beautiful red-headed girl. She could not replace her husband.

Mother and I settled in a small flat in New Steine, Brighton, but nothing seemed to stand still in our home for long.

One day, she and I were having tea in the Hotel Metropole in Brighton, when Mother suddenly gripped my arm and said: 'Look over there—that officer wearing Daddy's badge . . .'

Sure enough, I saw a young subaltern—very young—with fair hair and earnest blue eyes, sitting close to us talking to another officer. He was looking (so he joked at a later date) at my pretty mother, not at me. Mother went straight across to him and asked him point-blank if he had seen or heard of my step-father in the battle of Loos.

The young subaltern stood gravely to attention while she told him about Daddy. He was full of compassion but he couldn't help her. He had never met Captain Dealtry. He had not been in that terrible battle. Mother was resigned to this sort of disappointment. The boy shyly asked us to join him and his friend for tea.

This was Harry White—whom I later christened 'Billy', and 'Bill' to me he then remained. He became a great friend. We found that we were exactly the same age—only four days between us. He was a charming person; not sophisticated, but full of simplicity and a rare honesty which is not too easy to find. He came from Northamptonshire. His passion in life was cricket. As our friendship developed I found myself going to watch cricket matches with him, and learning to like it. The day was to come when I watched him play in a County Cricket Match for Northants against Sussex.

Billy was only one of 'Kitchener's lot', but he took a fancy to the army and after the war went out to India to serve as a regular officer with the Punjab Regiment. He was there for thirty years. He came home married to a beautiful girl named Rosamund. Now he has two sons of his own in the army and lives not far from me. We still meet. I remember him not only for the joyous friendship we shared when we were both nineteen, but for the fact that he was the only man in the world who thought that 'Denise' didn't suit me, so he renamed me 'Peggy'. My first husband called me 'Peggy', too, for a time. Today when I meet Bill White and hear that name, it sounds odd—as though it doesn't belong to me—then it sweeps me back into the past when I was so very young!

In 1916, two army officers—wartime soldiers—who had been seriously wounded in the Battle of the Somme, arrived in Brighton to convalesce. Both played an important part in the lives of my mother and myself. One of them was Sydney Groom, the schoolmaster who had been so devoted to Mother in Cornwall. His right leg was badly injured. He had been transferred to Brighton from Netley Hospital at Mother's request.

To Mother, Sydney was a link with her past happy life and his love for her had not changed. Although the memory of Berkeley would never really die, she gradually turned to Sydney for comfort—and found it.

I in my turn, found an interest in the other young officer. He was 1st Lieut. Arthur Howis Robins of the 2nd Essex Regiment, and the man whom I was eventually to marry. Like Sydney, he, too, had been severely wounded in the Battle of the Somme and had come home with a fractured femur and many complications.

I first met him at a party held by the officers in King Manuel's Convalescent Home on the Brighton front. Arthur had been sent there after a year in another hospital where he went through sixteen painful operations and nearly died of septicaemia. Those who were mobile danced. I adored dancing but willingly sat out with the tall fair young officer, who, to my great surprise, told me that he had originally joined the Artists Rifles and met my brother Adrian, so we had something in common to talk about. He had also, like Uncle Cosmo, been educated at Marlborough which gave us another topic for conversation. I had heard so much about Marlborough from Uncle Cosmo, and Arthur, his father and grandfather had all been there. After that, *the dansant*, Arthur came to my home regularly for tea, or took me out.

It was 1917. I had begun to work daily in a Red Cross Officers Home in Percival Terrace as a V.A.D. nurse.

Mother went on writing because we were very hard up. She had only the disgracefully inadequate pension that used to be given in those days to a Captain's widow.

Remembering it all, I am quite sure that my emotions at

this time were decidedly confused.

Like most girls I longed to find the right man and to get married. I was afraid I might die before the war ended and never experience the rapturous joy that my mother had felt for my step-father.

Several men drifted in and out of my life before I finally fell seriously in love with Arthur. Nothing before that seemed to last. My sentimental affair with the young captain in Daddy's battalion had already ended. I lived, as so many girls did during the war in that hectic, feverish atmosphere, falling in love—falling out again—never somehow finding the man who could hold my affections and stabilise my life.

At this time I was a gay, talkative, friendly sort of girl, but underneath the gaiety, there was a serious side. I didn't want promiscuous love-affairs. I wanted romance—but with it—security. Arthur was just a shy young man with charm. He was only twenty-two. He was very quiet at times but a good host—fond of going to the theatre or cinema and giving little parties. He looked at me with enormous blue eyes which held a curiously sad expression. (In years to come I was to become irritated by those large mild eyes because his expression rather bothered my conscience. It often made me feel that I must say 'yes' to him even if I wanted to say 'no'!)

He was tall—six foot. At the time of our first meeting he still walked with crutches. For the rest of his life one leg remained shorter than the other and he had to wear a built-up shoe. He was good-looking with the bright gold curling hair and fair complexion that distinguished most of the Robins. They came of good Yeoman stock with a touch of Huguenot some way back in the family history. I often thought the French strain showed itself quite definitely in Arthur. He had a markedly good taste in food and wines.

He and I got on well but it was only later that I began to take a real interest in him. By that time he was very much in love with me.

He had hitherto led a secluded country life in a remote village in Essex, and had never had a love affair. He found me unusual and a little wild (so he told me), and was intrigued, and alive to the fact that he wanted to marry me.

I was not sure of my feelings for him. Sometimes he was too quiet for me. But I admired his courage. He had to submit to frightful operations. He never complained. Often before his wound had healed, he would insist upon getting up. To everybody's surprise, even while he was still on crutches, he would walk for miles, or take part in a day's shooting.

He was a magnificent shot and sportsman—like his father. As a young boy before the war he was good at games. He refused to allow his lame leg to disable him. I often heard members of the shooting parties which he organised after the war, express their surprise that *he* didn't seem to get as tired as they did!

He was by no means artistic. He had no interest in reading or music. He once confessed to me that he only knew that *God Save The King* was being played when everybody stood up.

He introduced me to the world of sport which I knew little about. I listened enthralled to his tales of shooting and fishing. We used to meet in the garage behind the hospital where he kept his old two-seater car and a pair of ferrets in a cage, as he liked to go out rabbiting with the farmers. I remember sitting in this car with him, listening to the shuffling and squeaking of the ferrets. It doesn't sound romantic, but it was romance to me!

He would tell me about his Essex home and his favourite Sealyham, Donna, and the sad little Yorkshire terrier, Peggie, who had been his mother's favourite. She had lain down on his coat when he went away to the war, refusing food or comfort; and died there.

His father, Harry Robins, was on the Baltic—a grainbroker, as was Arthur's grandfather before him. Mrs. Robins, who had been a Miss Alice Sibthorpe, originally came from the village of Fryerning. Arthur was born there. They were a country-loving family. Later Arthur's parents moved to their Queen Anne farmhouse in the pretty village of Margaretting near Ingatestone. They stayed there for thirty years or more. Arthur had a brother, Vaughan, who was a year younger than himself, and also an older sister, Dorothy.

Once I got to know these Robins I began to realise why Arthur was so introverted. His father was a blustering hearty man with an unaccountably coarse streak. Early photographs show him as a handsome boy. When I met him he was extraordinarily like King George V with a brown beard and twinkling blue eyes. He had no interest in people. He gave his heart and most of his time to growing roses. A room full of silver cups and bowls testified to his skill. He won a prize every year at the Chelsea Rose Show. He lacked tolerance or sympathy for Arthur. He was jealous of the fact that Arthur's mother in her lifetime used to give most of her love to her shy elder son.

For Arthur, his mother's untimely death at the age of forty-two was a loss that hit him hard. After she had gone, he withdrew into his shell. I drew him out of it for a time—but not for long. Neither were things made better for him when Vaughan, known to the family as 'Goldie' on account of his bright curls when he was a small boy—also died young.

The deaths of the two people whom he most loved followed by constant quarrels and misunderstandings with his father affected him adversely. He laughed a lot, but his was a nervous laugh that masked painful embarrassment. He liked to play practical jokes; harmless, but in time madly irritating to me. Perhaps I took myself too seriously. I hated all the things that mattered most to me to be made a mock of by my husband.

However, for a time I imagined myself to be deeply in love with Arthur, and saw none of his faults. I set my heart upon becoming Mrs. Arthur Robins.

My mother, with more foresight and experience, assured me that I would be doing the wrong thing if I married Arthur. She was right, but it was largely her third marriage that encouraged me to rush into my own matrimonial venture.

On New Year's Day, in January, 1918, Mother said good-bye for ever to the ill-fated name of Dealtry. She was married to Sydney Groom in the Register Office at Brighton. By that time, like Arthur, Sydney was very lame but made light of it. He fully expected once he was demobilised to be able to go back to schoolmastering.

It is a disgraceful reflection on this country that it was a full two years, after answering hundreds of advertisements and writing hundreds of letters, before he found a job. Then it was not the Government that offered him one. Not a school would accept him because of his war wound—and the fact that he could not take part in *games*. His scientific brain and knowledge counted for nothing. Hardly an attractive reward for a young man's patriotism!

Later on, he did well, however, and in 1930, became a Lecturer in the Science Museum in Kensington from which post he eventually retired with an M.B.E. in 1958.

I was not happy about Mother's marriage at first, but Sydney finally proved himself a wonderful husband. He gave her all the care and devotion which she needed once her health failed. To him she never really grew old but remained the beautiful charming woman who had first fascinated him down in Newquay.

With him, she led a quiet life—very different from the series of stormy adventures she had shared with her ill-fated Berkeley.

She wrote only spasmodically, but when she was seventy-five she actually launched into thrillers which were published under the name of K. C. Groom. A wonderful achievement.

Arthur Robins and I were the witnesses in the Register Officer on that cold New Year's morning when she married Sydney.

He, poor man, was embarrassed by a fiendish cold and could scarcely make the responses.

I watched this union with mixed feelings. I seemed fated to be deprived of Mother's companionship. I felt that only for those two brief years following Daddy's death had she really belonged to me, and that I was the daughter she loved. But once again she was to be taken from me. She was the truly feminine type of woman who needs a man in her life. And now that I am older I am more understanding of her needs. She took it for granted, of course, that it would not be long before I, myself, would be married.

The Registrar—an old man—shook hands with me, looked

at the tall, fair young man in uniform at my side and joked:

'Ah ha! I wouldn't be surprised if you two aren't the next.'

We were.

Shortly after Mother settled down with her third husband to a life of retirement, Arthur and I became engaged.

He took me down to Essex to meet his family and see his home for the first time.

I wore a ring on my finger; an inexpensive half-hoop with a single sapphire and two small diamonds. It was the best Arthur could afford. He had only his subaltern's pay—no private means. He was afraid from the start that he had nothing much to offer me and that he would not be able to make me happy.

I was, however, blindly in love. I refused to be parted from him.

How sad that romantic love can die so quickly if it is not backed up by vision—and by basic understanding and friendship.

It would be wrong for me to blame Arthur because eventually I was disappointed in him. He was a simple man. I was a creative artist, full of complexities. I demanded too much. Arthur was unable to live up to my conception of love and marriage.

From the start our footsteps were dogged by a series of misunderstandings, and my rose-coloured spectacles were quickly smashed, but I was full of confidence when I first went down to Margaretting to make the acquaintance of my future-in-laws.

PART TWO

1

THE Robins family lived in a lovely old Queen Anne farm-house called 'Ponders' which stands on the London to Chelms-ford road, half hidden by trees. Today, the heavy traffic thunders up and down and it must be very noisy. When I first went there it was quiet and secluded; hardly a car was to be seen on the road. Arthur's father used a horse and trap for transport. The fat pony ambled daily, lazily, to Chelmsford Station where Mr. Robins caught his business train to Liver-pool Street.

I only saw 'Ponders' after its former 'glory' had departed (so Arthur informed me). It had been darkened first by the early death of his mother—then the war. Once it was a cheer-ful, busy household and there was much entertaining. There were garden-parties, dinners and cricket every Saturday on the Village green—the Robins were firm supporters of the local club, and old Robins captained the team. Arthur's mother used to give the cricket teas; later on his step-mother presided. I can see those long trestle-tables under the trees, spread with white cloths, heaped with buns and cakes; a great urn of tea ready for the thirsty cricketers.

In 1918, the once-beautiful grounds looked sadly neglected. Only the roses which old Harry Robins grew with such artis-try, remained to testify to his pre-war horticultural triumphs.

Arthur's mother had been replaced by a step-mother whom Arthur and his brother strongly resented. They called her Aimée. The Old Man had married her too quickly after their mother's death for their liking. The villagers were still talking about the late Mrs. Robins—what a wonderful horsewoman she was—how good with children and animals, how much be-loved. I heard that towards the end of her life she unfortunately did not get on with her husband. Both of them had flaming tempers.

The second Mrs. Robins was a plump cheerful woman with fine eyes and a soft amiable disposition. She was full of the desire to please. It was unfortunate for her that Arthur and his brother disliked her. Old Robins often treated Aimée as a menial. He teased her remorselessly because of her ample proportions and large appetite.

I can see him now, leaning across the table in their long, low dining-room, full of rich mahogany furniture, and with fine paintings of former Robinses on the red-papered walls—growling at poor old Aimée.

'*Killing yourself with your teeth!*' he would jeer at her and shout with glee because she crimsoned and hung her head. She would continue to eat, her spaniel-like eyes beseeching for the tolerance and understanding which she never received from the family. They tried to crush her spirit. The one happiness in her life was the little daughter born soon after the marriage—Enid.

Arthur had a slightly snobbish streak. I think he was a little ashamed of the state of his old home, and of the deterioration of his father; and angry because his mother had been replaced so quickly. He became morose and more silent than usual when we went down to 'Ponders'.

Harry Robins had of course changed greatly with the years. He was impoverished and shabby. He had cut out all entertaining. Nobody came to the house. He used to say that the war had ruined him but he was a bit of a skinflint and disliked spending what he did possess.

The house was falling into decay. There were only oil lamps and candles when I first went there, no modern luxuries. I, myself, had not been accustomed to luxury, but I remember walking around 'Ponders' with my fiancé, feeling horrified at the melancholy condition of that once fine old place. There were still lovely things to admire—antiques and Georgian silver which had been collected by Great-Uncle Howis Robins who used to be a famous auctioneer in the Dickens' period, and was a connoisseur. The carpets needed patching. The curtains were faded and the covers had shrunk. The bath in the one old-fashioned bathroom was rusted up. The hot water system constantly broke down. No one seemed to care. If Aimée timidly suggested calling in a plumber she was told to take a cold bath and like it.

The Old Man himself had an icy shower every morning—he didn't like hot water so the rest of us had to be content with cans of water heated by Aimée and poured into a hip-bath by her little village daily maid.

The kitchen was large, cold and draughty. Aimée did all the cooking. There really was a sad 'end of the war' atmosphere at 'Ponders'.

Out of doors it was just as depressing. In the kennels there were two dogs—both very old—one dying of tumour. He should have long since been put to sleep, but one of Old Man Robins' fetishes was a refusal to have any animal destroyed. He believed it should be left to die when and how nature decided.

He was so loth to spend money that he would not even pay for his little daughter Enid to go to a good school.

When I first saw Enid, she was a thin sad-eyed child, but in his way the Old Man adored her and he was also in time to prove a charming and friendly grandfather to my family. His character was full of contradictions.

He spent a fortune on his rose bushes. There was an acre of them. He kept them in perfect condition, and was continually spraying, budding and creating new species. He used to get up early every morning to attend to them and continued doing so, until a few days before he died.

After meeting me he openly expressed his disapproval. Arthur was wrong, he said, to be marrying the 'artistic type'.

'You're a fool, Arthur,' he said. 'You should have chosen a woman who can cook and sew.'

I was highly incensed. This was the beginning of many years of antagonism between me and my father-in-law, but I liked the friendly, down-trodden step-mother and often ranged myself on her side against the Robins family. She was at least human. I began to think *they* were not!

Arthur's young brother was away in the R.F.C. The only other member of the family at home was the sister, Dorothy— golden-haired and blue-eyed like them all. She made the best meringues I have ever eaten in my life. She prepared her father's roses for exhibition at the shows with great skill and artistry. She was always nice to me, but by the time I met her she had become repressed and saddened by the untimely loss of her own mother. She found life boring and depressing in that ruined house.

A couple of years later she married William Hanworth, a schoolmaster who had once been billeted at 'Ponders'. As an army officer he was stationed in the district. After the war he took a job in a college in Cairo. He and Dorothy lived there for many years.

They had two sons; both have done well.

Two things connected with my initial entrée into that strange household stand out in my memory. Firstly, the amazing fact that there was not a single book in the house. Nobody read. I found only a dusty pile of gardening annuals when I looked for a novel to take to bed.

Of course the warning bell should have sounded for me then, but I was still too much in love to take a sensible survey. Besides which, Arthur seemed so sad and lonely and out of tune with his own people, I felt that he needed me as much as I needed him. If anything, the unhappy atmosphere of his old home challenged me. I felt I must make him happy and build a really lovely home for him.

The second revelation was my discovery of a Bechstein grand piano in the drawing-room. I opened the lid delightedly and asked who played. My future father-in-law grinned at me wickedly:

'Nobody. We're not musicians down here.'

'Then why have you got a piano?' I asked him.

He roared with laughter.

'It was going cheap in a sale and looks a nice piece of furniture—well, doesn't it?'

I was thunderstruck. I had never come across anything like this before. I sat down and played the beautiful Bechstein, comforted by the richness of its tone. Arthur liked me to play and sing even though he had no idea to what he was listening.

Mother had settled down in Brighton as Mrs. Sydney Groom. Arthur and I returned there having received Mr. Robins' somewhat unwilling blessing. The war dragged on; Brighton was still crammed with soldiers; the wounded being wheeled up and down the front in their long spinal carriages, officers and men on crutches; khaki, khaki everywhere and the end not yet in sight.

When Arthur was demobilised he came out with nothing but his wound gratuity and a pension of about eighty-five pounds a year. He had various operations in the future. The septic wound left by that fracture never really healed.

Now nothing and nobody could keep us apart.

We were married on the 15th June, 1918, the same year of my mother's re-marriage.

2

Now that I look back through the years—and it does seem a long way back to 1918—I find it rather melancholy to remember all those hopes and dreams that were gradually to fade. During any war, caught up in the fever and drama, emotions are apt to become exaggerated. It wasn't a good time for calm speculation. I so longed for a home of my own after the constant changes and insecurities of my old life, I'm afraid I did not use much judgement.

Marriages, of course, can go wrong even when they are carefully planned. The shadow of divorce had darkened a good many bridals. Today, of course, I know that there are three insurances for a successful marriage. Common interests. Sexual harmony. Understanding.

Arthur and I proved incompatible from the start. I was disappointed even at the end of our first fortnight together. But for a long time I refused to face up to the fact that I had chosen the wrong man.

For a short time we occupied furnished rooms in Brighton. Then a few months after our marriage I discovered that I was pregnant.

I was pleased but Arthur was troubled. We had no home and it seemed to him all too quick and rather improvident. He wrote to his father who invited us to stay at 'Ponders' until we found a permanent home.

I didn't want to live in the Robins' gloomy old house, but there seemed nothing else for it. Down to Margaretting we went. I was beginning to feel sick. When carrying my babies, I could hardly keep down any food during the first three or four months. This made me dispirited, but I was delighted that I was going to be a mother. I hoped that I would find a tremendous link with, and joy in, a child of my own.

But not even having a baby could bring Arthur and myself close together. We were both too young, too self-centred and inexperienced to make a go of things. I was soon to learn the bitter truth of Byron's words: *'Man's love is of man's life a thing apart; 'Tis woman's whole existence.'*

It was a fatal move going down to live in Arthur's old home. Young newly-married couples should live by themselves.

Aimée was pathetically glad to see me. She did all she could for me but my father-in-law, pleased though he was that he was about to be made a grandfather, showed no more gentleness than usual, or personal affection for me. He didn't understand me. I was too emotional for him. He was a harsh realist. I cried often and he thought me a fool. However, I was not the type to be easily crushed and at times I battled with him furiously. I was disappointed because Arthur refused to take my side. He would sit silent, eyes downcast, an embarrassed smile on his lips while the Old Man and I held our disputes. I felt that my own husband should have been ready to jump up and defend me from the world. He was obviously afraid of his father and always had been. I felt let down by this attitude.

Life seemed a bit worse at 'Ponders' than before. The Old Man who used to be such a gourmet had become mean about food. The war was still on—prices were rising, of course, and meat and butter scarce. We often ate nothing for supper but porridge and a few fried tomatoes to follow. It didn't seem to hurt me—or my coming baby—which proves that we all eat too much.

Nobody came to the house. Mr. Robins had become anti-social. My only excitement was to drive with Arthur in the old pony trap into Chelmsford to look at the shops, and the cricket teas in the weekends.

I can still feel the cold gloom of 'Ponders'—especially of Arthur's and my bedroom. It had a very low ceiling in which the plaster had cracked and the whitewash browned. A single candle was the only light, throwing grotesque shadows on that sinister ceiling. I used to lie in the big old-fashioned double-bed and stare up at them. It wasn't easy to preserve the warmth and glamour of love in that atmosphere. I began to feel mentally and emotionally starved.

There were, however, amusing moments; one unforgettable occasion when the Old Man lost his temper (what a temper it was!) because he could not find a particular cricket shirt which he wanted before a cricket match.

Arthur, Aimée, Enid and I were in the garden. It was a warm August day. The Old Man leaned out of his window and demanded his shirt. Aimée went in to look for it but couldn't find it and came downstairs crimson with mortification.

Pandemonium followed. The Old Man pulled out every drawer, emptied every cupboard, and flung the things, one after the other, into the garden. The lawn below was strewn with every possible article of a gentleman's clothing. As he dropped each one, he thrust out his bearded face and with a snarl of rage, shouted:

'Pick that up, you fool—and that—and that—*and that*!'

Arthur, as usual, remained silent and disdainful. Aimée was in tears; little Enid stared goggle-eyed. When Aimée started to walk towards the lawn, I drew her back.

'You're *not* to pick up all those things. Don't you do it. Let him pick them up himself. Leave them there.'

But of course she wouldn't. She was much too scared of him. We picked the things up together and carried them upstairs. By this time the Old Man was dressed. He always looked so sleek and immaculate in his white flannels, and with his beard freshly trimmed. His violent temper had subsided. At the sight of Aimée staggering in with so many of his garments, he roared with laughter.

'That'll teach you to lose my shirts!'

What a character he was! However unpleasant at the time, I have to smile about it in retrospect, but I could only endure four months at 'Ponders', then after a particularly bitter scene with the Old Man, I told Arthur we must leave. He was upset, but saw my point of view. I had begun to be so unhappy. I couldn't face that cold unfriendly house one day longer. Things came to a head on the day when I was told that an old spaniel bitch about to whelp was not to be allowed to keep even one of her puppies, because they had a mongrel father. Feeling particularly in sympathy with the spaniel at the time, I pleaded for her. The pups were drowned by the unsympathetic old man Robins in front of my very eyes—as soon as they were born. He scoffed at my distress. Even Arthur called me stupidly soft. It was the last straw. I felt heartbroken and alien to the whole Robins' family.

I think Arthur realised then that he must do something drastic if he was to keep me. I was already proving too incomprehensibly tempestuous and rebellious for him. We both suffered. We left Essex and started life again in London.

Arthur was offered a job on the Baltic at a salary of five pounds a week. We found a little flat (for fifty pounds a year) at the top of a cheap block of flats in Maida Vale. We moved in just before November 11th—Armistice Day.

We managed to furnish our first home by buying cheap furniture and my father-in-law, who seemed to bear me no malice because I had quarrelled with him, gave us some things from 'Ponders'. He pitied Arthur but did not turn his back on us. We also spent the money we had accumulated out of our wedding cheques.

So hard up were we that I had to do without a dressing table until Arthur, who was a good carpenter, made me one, using two tea chests to which I nailed a cretonne-frilled curtain!

Armistice Day brought blissful relief to us—just as it did to millions. Wild hysteria swept through London that day and I shall never forget one moment of fear when I thought my unborn baby might be harmed.

Arthur had taken me to celebrate by having tea in a hotel in the West End. Suddenly some waiters, looking scared, rushed into the lounge and asked everybody to leave. They told us that the manager had ordered all tables and chairs to be collected and stacked away.

A vast crowd was milling through the streets, banging at the closed doors of hotels and restaurants, demanding refreshment. It looked like being a celebration all right! Before we knew where we were, we were in a screaming laughing mass of people who had surged into the lounge.

For a few moments I was jostled in the crowd. Arthur put a protective arm around me and with the help of a waiter, hustled me through a back door out into the street.

We managed to reach the underground and get home. We spent the night in our little flat listening to the sound of shouting, laughing and singing. It went on all through the night.

Christmas was quiet, but although peace had come there was trouble ahead for the country. The cost of living rocketed. The prospect seemed gloomy. There was political unrest now. The terrible war had left its mark.

I settled down to my new life and tried to feel more resigned to the disappointment of my marriage.

Arthur had many fine qualities. I admired these, and even in the far-off future, after our marriage ended, I was aware of his essential integrity. He was one of the bravest men I ever met. It was the curiously stubborn quality in him and his hopelessly prejudiced outlook on people and things in general which finally killed my love. But when he controlled that awful urge of his to ridicule everything that I liked, I was fond of him.

I did not mind being hard up but found my life had begun to be a little boring, so I started to write again. In my spare time I knew I could make some money which was sorely needed.

I felt lonely all day while Arthur was at the office but looked forward eagerly to the birth of our first child. There was no question of my going into a hospital or having a special *accoucheur*. I went to an old G.P. in the district—a dear old man—and we engaged the services of a mid-wife who was to come 'when the pains began'.

Twice every day I climbed four flights of stairs. I grew larger and more breathless. I did the shopping and tried hard to make ends meet at a time when everything was exorbitant. Butter was rationed and expensive. Meat, too, was dear. Most wives in my social circle in those days had a maid but I could not afford one and did my own work entirely.

My mother arrived on the scene, anxious to help me, and took a furnished flat in a block near ours. I saw her every day. We got along better than usual. My sister-in-law, Dorothy, volunteered to come up from Essex and cook for me while I was in bed. The Old Man did his bit and occasionally sent us game after a day's shooting, or a chicken.

Before I met Arthur, I used to keep a record of the sales or rejections of my manuscripts, with the prices paid for stories sold. I looked through my accounts book just before Eve was born, and noted that I used to receive twenty-five shillings a week from Dundee for writing a series of short stories with titles like 'Nell of the Coffee Stall', 'The Captain's Daughter', 'Kid, The Waif'. D. C. Thomson were still keen on tales about ill-treated slum-children.

I also saw that I had earned thirty shillings a week writing for a paper called *Girl's Weekly*, the same for a hospital-nurse series, 'Nurse Rose of the Ward' which was taken by the *Weekly Welcome*.

It is interesting to note (forty-eight years later) that Hospital Nurse novels are still so very popular with women's magazines readers.

I made up my mind that as soon as I could afford domestic help, I would set aside a regular time for writing.

I may have made a mistake in my marriage but I was not going to make another by wasting my talents as a writer.

It was just a question now, it seemed, of opportunity.

D.R., aged 4, with mother

D.R. at 11

Myself, aged 19, as V.A.D. in
First World War

Neill, 1939. Armband initials stand for Instructor Fire Control

Our Wedding Day—30th October 1939

Roland Pertwee—author, and
my greatest friend
Left: Michael, his son, who
has written the foreword to
this book

The Sutton family (daughter F
From left to right: Murray, Rosa
and her husband Milan, and Ann

The Chadwick family (daughter Anne)
From left to right: Pippa, Pauline-
Belinda, myself, and Anne

Pat with my grandson Graeme

The Clark family (daughter Pat)

My grandson Iain Campbell-Clark

My grand-daughter Nicola Campbell-Clark

Annabel Sutton,
my grand-daughter

My eldest daughter, Eve

R.N.A. Dinner 1963, Barbara Cartland at 'mike'. 'The President', myself, between Ian Fleming and Russell Braddon

First R.N.A. Dinner. *From left to right:* John Attenborough, myself, A. P. Herbert, Alex Stuart, Bill Smith

With Neill on holiday at Pollensa, Majorca

With Paul Hodder-Williams, the Chairman of Hodder and Stoughton, at an office party

3

EVE, my first child, was born on the 31st March, 1919.

I had started labour at eleven o'clock on the previous night. I think I climbed too many stairs up to the flat where Mother and Sydney were living and with whom we were playing bridge. Then I had to climb many more stairs to reach our own flat.

The infant decided to arrive—one week early.

Arthur could not find a taxi in the early hours of that morning and had to walk, wounded-leg and all, halfway across London to Chelsea to fetch my monthly nurse. She was not on the telephone. Neither were we.

Mother rushed around and took charge. She was always very resourceful at such times and made a good nurse.

I helped to make my bed and prepare everything. Each time the pain grew worse, I consoled myself by the thrilling thought of this child who was going to be such a wonderful innovation, and mean so much in my life.

I suffered for fourteen gruelling hours and only in the last few minutes when the doctor arrived, was I allowed a whiff of chloroform. Finally it was all over. Mother was very proud of herself because she had helped with the birth of her new grandchild. I recovered consciousness to be told by her that I had a little daughter of my own.

Many, many times since then, I have been asked by the Press:

'What is the most exciting thing that has ever happened to you?'

I always give the same answer:

'The moment when they put my baby in my arms. Suddenly she opened her eyes and looked straight up into mine—and it was almost as though she recognised me.'

It is true. No thrill of the future ever exceeded that one. It seemed so incredible that this tiny thing with her bright blue eyes, perfect hands and feet and soft gold hair—she had lots of it for an infant—was alive and *mine*. I was the happiest girl in the world. The pains were forgotten. I asked for Arthur and wanted to show her to him. I was distinctly put out when told that he had long since gone to the City after being assured that all was likely to go well with me. I suppose I had always, in my dramatic way, imagined that one's husband should pace up and down outside the door, sweating with fear—torn with anguish for his suffering wife.

But there was nothing like that about Arthur as I was soon to discover. He was immensely kind and sympathetic at times, but to use his own words—*child-birth is a natural event. Why fuss?* It was just another disillusionment for me, but I was happy once he finally came home, kissed me and admired his pretty little daughter.

I don't think I shall ever forget the old 'gamp' who looked after me during that first week. She used to sit beside my bed singing while she bathed the baby. Eve was the prettiest she had ever seen, she declared. Her Cockney twanging voice obviously fascinated the infant who stared up at her.

'*Beautiful Katy! K-K-K-Katy! ...*'

One of the popular songs of the moment. It made me laugh, but 'Katy' was certainly not to be my baby's name. I chose Eve for her. She was the 'first woman'. Her second name, was Louise after Louise Whitlock, a convent friend who became her godmother.

Once I was up and about again, Dorothy returned to her own home, Mother went back to Brighton, and I had to manage alone. I found that the housework and cooking, plus a baby, occupied all my time. I despaired of every finding a moment in which to get down to my literary work. I fed Eve myself, but was very inexperienced and in 1919 there were no instructive clinics for ignorant mothers. I had to practise on my poor baby. Often I failed to do the right thing. A fair amount of screaming in protest followed, added to which I didn't like having to climb all those stairs. She soon grew too heavy and I hated having to push her pram through the dreary sooty precincts of Paddington Recreation Grounds. It was the only open space anywhere near our block.

Being a wife and mother seemed to me all very well but

where was romance? The joy and hope of discovering real happiness seemed to be seeping out of my life.

Arthur did his best, but he knew little about being a husband and was not interested in fatherhood. We began to lapse into long silences and hardly spoke. We just didn't have anything to say to each other.

I chafed against this régime. I longed for companionship of the right kind and for leisure in which to write and use my brain. With horror I anticipated long years stretching ahead when I would do nothing but push the pram round Paddington Recreation Grounds, wash nappies and cook. I knew to my cost that I was not by nature very domesticated and could not be content without some intellectual interest.

One day I bought a copy of a paper called *Forget-me-not Novels* (price 2d.). It was one of the most popular publications from the Amalgamated Press during those post-war days.

I read the long complete story feeling slight disdain—it seemed so poor. If they wanted romance, I told myself, I could write something better than this. But *when*? *When* could I find time to write?

I owned an old typewriter but had no *time*. That was the trouble. After Arthur came home and supper was washed up, I was too tired to write. I despaired. I was sure if I could once get a foot on the bottom rung of the ladder, I would soon climb it. I *knew* I was capable of hard work. I could earn regular money and so help Arthur with the household expenses. We would be able to leave this flat, find a more suitable home, and begin to *live*. This present life was to me a bare existence.

Of course, in the bottom of my heart I knew that it all seemed worse because I was no longer in love with my husband. If we had been more in tune, I could have put up with the struggle. But I had reached a pitch when I felt that I must re-shape my existence. It was not my nature to sit down and allow misfortune to conquer me—so I set to work to get out of the rut.

That night, I had a long talk with Arthur. I got out my little old accounts book and proved to him that I could make money regularly if given the opportunity.

This was when he turned up trumps. He was most helpful. He, himself, was finding the financial burden heavy. He agreed that it would be foolish not to harness my money-making capacity.

It was June.

Eve was then three months old. She was a peevish baby but thrived, and grew into a beautiful child. I felt I had done something terrific by producing such a gorgeous little creature! I wanted money in order to dress her attractively (as well as myself!). I wanted *her* to have a chance. It was stifling hot in our top flat during the summer months. It was no place for a baby. We could, of course, always go down and stay at 'Ponders'. But remembering my past disagreements with father-in-law and the gloom and decay, I was not over anxious to live there again. Arthur, at last, agreed. He made me an offer. His wound-gratuity was still in the bank untouched. He had been storing it up for a rainy day. Seeing the state of my mind, he decided that the rain had come! First, he said, he would take me down to Cornwall, where we had a standing invitation to stay with Elsie Moffat—my mother's former maid. She was now Mrs. Percy Evans and lived in a cottage in St. Columb Minor, not far from my mother's old home.

Arthur was entitled to ten days' holiday. The Cornish air would benefit the baby as well as me. He could go bass fishing off the rocks, which he would enjoy. We would all be happy there.

Then when we came home again, he would make me an allowance out of his gratuity. I could get a daily cook and a living-in nursemaid. In those days domestic help was cheap, although in our position, it all seemed madly extravagant. But I flung my arms around my husband's neck, hugged him joyfully and accepted his offer. I would pay him back, I promised. He would see—it would be worthwhile.

Just how worthwhile it was to prove neither of us dreamed.

I realise now that I owe my subsequent success to my own self-confidence, a useful vanity that I had inherited from my father—and to Arthur's faith in me.

We had our Cornish holiday. I remember well that eight-hour journey from Paddington to Newquay.

Eve, as a baby, was a poor sleeper. She woke easily. I dreaded having to hold her and try to pacify her, and knew that her crying would also annoy our fellow passengers. So we asked the guard's permission to travel in the luggage van where we could fix up Eve's Treasure Cot. She would feel more at home in that and I would also have privacy in which to nurse her.

I can see so plainly those two harassed young parents seated uncomfortably, side by side, on a couple of trunks while the infant—comfortable in her cot—slept most of the journey. The shrill hoot of an express rushing in the opposite direction made her wake with a start, and burst into tears. But on the whole, it was a good journey for her, if a back-breaking one for us!

We arrived at St. Columb Minor. I was thrilled to see the blue translucent sea and the broad brown beach of Porth again.

Elsie was overjoyed to see her 'Miss Denise' and what she called the 'lil ole baby'. Dear Elsie!—she generously looked after Eve for me during those ten days which gave me a real rest.

I was intrigued to walk down the hill from Elsie's cottage and look at Porth Bean after so long. I remembered all the joys and sorrows I had experienced there in Mother's once beloved house. She, too, had known happiness—and grief— with her Berkeley there.

It was morbid to dwell on the past and remember that Daddy was dead—blown to pieces. Better to think that she was now Mrs. Sydney Groom, and that I was married and a mother. But I was depressed to remember the bitter tears I had shed while I lived in that beautiful old house. Strangely enough a kind of glamour also lingered there; the bitter-sweet memory of my mother, so beautiful and lively then, wearing one of her long graceful dresses, sitting at the Bluthner piano singing to Daddy, Uncle Cosmo—and me.

> *Summer, summer must you go*
> *For two of us have loved you so . . .*

Never sunshine, never rain
Will fall on just we two again!...

One of Lyell-Taylor's sentimental ballads which had been her great favourite. It was as well she had not realised then that all too soon there would be no more sunshine, no more rain for Berkeley.

When we got back to London I engaged a little maid, and a nurse for Eve. Easy enough to find in those days, and for a reasonable wage. Now at last I had time to sit down at my old Remington and begin to write for my living.

I typed away most of the day, and half the evening.

When Arthur came back from the Baltic, he found me still tapping out a story—full of enthusiasm, if hardly able to see, my eyes were so tired. During the days ahead, he was often to come home like that and find his wife feverishly working, struggling to establish herself as a romance writer.

It was a gamble—but for me a definite challenge. I've always been a gambler and I was determined to win. I would establish myself in the women's magazine world and Arthur should get back the money he was rather anxiously taking out of his precious savings.

What would happen if I failed; and nothing remained for the 'rainy day'? That was an anxiety of course. We had absolutely nobody in the world to help us should be get into difficulties. Arthur would sooner have died than ask his father for money and in any case the Old Man was far from affluent, and my mother was still having to write and help Sydney who had not yet found a permanent job. *And* there was Eve.

We had so looked forward to showing her to Arthur's brother, Goldie, who was her godfather. I had met him before my marriage when he was on leave from his squadron. He had already won the D.F.C. and was a most popular young man; fair and blue-eyed like the rest of the Robins' family and very gay. He was much better able to stand up to his father than Arthur. Alas, Eve was never to know her Uncle Goldie.

All this time while Arthur and I were struggling to make ends meet Goldie had been working in Malaya on a rubber estate.

102

He had done well and wrote happy letters. His father adored him and we were all looking forward to his return.

He wrote to us telling us about all the presents he was bringing and what fun it would be to see his god-daughter for the *first* time. Then suddenly Arthur and I received a telegram from Aimée telling us to come home at once, and passing on the terrible news that Goldie was dead. He had died of some mysterious complaint on board ship. The Captain had cabled Mr. Robins. That was all that was so far known.

Arthur and I rushed down to 'Ponders'. We found the Old Man completely broken, sobbing his heart out. He had prepared a great welcome home for Goldie, his favourite son. A ham hung from the rafters in the kitchen. There were pheasants and partridges in the larder. Their friends had been asked to a celebration party.

Unknown to us, Goldie had not been well when he left Singapore on a Japanese liner. We heard afterwards from an English hospital nurse who was travelling in an unofficial capacity on the same boat, that Goldie had caught a chill on the kidney. The Japanese ship's doctor made a wrong and fatal diagnosis. He treated Goldie for a liver infection. Nephritis soon followed.

Twenty-four hours before the poor boy died, the English nurse went down to his cabin to see him. She was shocked and thought that his condition looked moribund. She asked an English doctor, also a passenger, to look at him but this doctor, bound by the red-tape of his profession, refused to interfere with the ship's doctor. This Jap eventually called upon the Englishman for help. By that time it was too late.

Goldie died just before the ship docked at Suez. His body was taken off there and buried in the English Cemetery. Dorothy was living with her husband and children in Cairo. She and Billy had arranged to meet the boat and go aboard for lunch with Goldie. Instead they had to make arrangements for Goldie's funeral; a terrible thing.

After the war ended when I was first out in Egypt, I drove to the English Cemetery in Suez and there read the inscription on the stone marking poor Goldie's grave: '*Harry Vaughan Robins*'.

I thought how sad, how terrible to die like that through a medical error of judgement—*and* red-tape. To die aged twenty-eight after coming through a terrible war without a scratch, and with a distinguished record of flying.

Arthur felt the loss of his brother keenly.

Our lives were rather overshadowed by this tragedy but we both went on working. I wrote furiously, determined to 'get on'.

I finished my first 'novelette' of twenty thousand words in two-and-a-half days; re-typed it, and sent it to the editor of *Forget-me-not Novels*, Fleetway House.

Now came the tense period of waiting—alternating between wild hope and despair—the awful fear that I had spent all that money on domestic help without justification.

At any moment the postman might shove a long narrow envelope through the letter-box; my rejected manuscript. I could hardly bear the idea.

I waited for three long weeks. I made myself ill with worry. Arthur, as always, remained silent and kept his thoughts to himself. Only Eve grew plump and pink and was happy, cooing and dimpling at me as though to reassure me that everything would be all right.

Came the wonderful morning when I received a letter from the Amalgamated Press—signed by a certain Mr. William Groves. (He would still be remembered by a few of the older generation who worked at A.P. in the 1920s.) It was to tell me that he had read my novelette entitled *The Artist's Model* and accepted it.

He was willing to pay me the sum of ten pounds. That was poor pay even in 1919, heaven knows! But to me it seemed a fortune. It was terrific news. Best of all to me seemed the last paragraph in that letter:

'*I'd like you to come and see me about future work. I could do with that sort of story regularly.*'

I went mad with excitement. I couldn't wait for Arthur to come home. When he did, I showed him the letter. I cried:

'I'm in! *I'm in!* We're going to be all right!'

Of course he was delighted. Now I felt that the wages of the 'daily' and the nursemaid, could go on being paid without conscience. Now, I felt that I really had started my career.

And that was, in fact, how it all began.

4

FROM that day onward I set out to work hard and consolidate my position. I still had uncomfortable leanings towards writing of a more intellectual kind and wanted recognition of some literary merit, but in my position then, there could be no place for grandiose ideas. I had to write for my bread and butter. I wasn't going to find it too hard, because what they needed in women's magazines was passion and romance. I could produce both. Because my marriage had, in so many respects, failed, and I was still hungry for the right kind of love, I poured my heart and soul into my books.

I went to see Mr. Groves.

I was scared both of him and the huge offices of Fleetway House Publications. I remember so vividly that first visit—myself, aged twenty-two, excited, trembling, apprehensive, listening while the Editor of *Forget-me-not Novels* told me how and what to write for him.

As I look back to 1919, I remember thinking rightly that day that it would be a long tiring climb before I reached the top of the ladder.

I began to write one novelette a week. That would bring in £10 a week. My husband's salary was then about eight pounds so we were positively well-off compared with our beginning.

Soon I was writing under three *nom-de-plumes*. I had also found a market for my stuff with the Allied Press and Newnes. I wrote for *Poppy's Paper*, *Peg's Paper*, *Weekend Novels* and many other magazines. I wrote so much that it couldn't all be published under one name.

I still have those early publications. I'm really quite surprised by the variety of these efforts; by 'Denise Chesterton'—'Eve Vaill'—'Anne Llewellyn'—my pseudonyms.

I couldn't write fast enough. I supplied the emotional fast-moving story that was so badly wanted. My early training in Dundee, and the example of my mother's experience in serial writing, stood me in good stead. Soon I developed a technique and style of my own. I found myself in constant demand by the editors of half a dozen or more periodicals.

At the same time, of course, I put up my price. Arthur suddenly found himself married to a woman whose old account books record that she made £538. 17s. 6d. in 1920. The annual figures were higher in 1921, and soon rose to £700. By 1924, I was making just under a thousand a year.

I had not yet published my first novel, but for a while the serial market kept me fully occupied. I discovered that I could write a long, strong romantic story full of quick moving drama, and luckily could turn such stories out at an unbelievable rate. I often wrote ten thousand words a day, typing madly with four fingers. (I had never been taught 'touchtyping'.)

My old account books are something of a revelation. Opening it at random today I see odd titles such as:

'Caught in a web' (sold to *Betty's Paper*)
'Passion's Prisoner' (sold to *Betty's Paper*)
'Forbidden Love', serial (sold to *Pam's Paper* for £128)

These and other 'Long Completes' for papers now obsolete, such as *Handy Stories*, *Woman's Friend*, *Bow Bells*, *Ideas*, pages and pages of my sales to these are recorded.

One of the most exciting articles written about me was one published in *The People* with a photograph of me in the centre of the page and the title: '£1 A WEEK GIRL WINS FAME AT LAST'.

This preceded the first newspaper serial I ever wrote and it was for this Sunday paper with its great circulation, which naturally made me very proud—for sure enough I *had* started by earning only a pound a week.

I seemed to have the strength to work at an increasing pace both before and after the birth of two more daughters. Nothing stopped me. Arthur benefited by what I was able to put into the 'kitty'. I don't think he really liked it. He was not the type to enjoy taking money from a woman. It disappointed me because he did not really appreciate my success.

Now that I am older and more tolerant, I can see things from his point of view as well as my own. But I found it irritating then because he would not share my triumph.

It was a good point in Arthur's character that he did not like his wife to pay the bills, but unfortunately it bred a kind of resentment and bitterness in him. Continual bickering and misunderstanding widened the gap between us.

More than ever I began to want not only a real lover, but a sympathetic companion—someone who could read the books I wrote, and upon whose critical faculty I could rely.

Arthur had no interest in my stories. He was engrossed with his own job. I flung myself into *my* work, and we moved from the flat where Eve had been born and went down to Brighton. Mother was there, also several of my old friends.

While we looked for a house we stayed in furnished rooms in Clifton Road. There I discovered that I was to have another child—rather too soon for my liking or for Arthur's pocket. We decided to stay in this place until after the baby arrived.

So my second daughter, Patricia Denise, was born in 1921. All the time I was waiting I kept thinking how nice it would be to have this child on my own birthday. It looked so likely.

On January 31st, Nurse Broad (she became a firm friend), who had been engaged to look after me, took me shopping. While in a chemist's shop I felt the first niggle of pain in my back. Nurse bustled me home in a taxi.

After a difficult and painful labour of twelve hours, my second daughter made her appearance, and sure enough, she came at four a.m. on 1st February, *my* birthday. The pains were fierce. I had no anaesthetic and I thought *'This is the last time!'*

Pat proved to be a strong-minded impetuous girl and her

entry into the world was certainly both strong *and* impetuous.

I was disappointed that she was not a son but my Aunt Alice forecast the infant's horoscope and prophesied that Pat would grow up to resemble me in many ways, and that she would end by becoming one of my best friends (which, indeed, she is!).

Considering the fact that I had my portable typewriter on my bed and finished an instalment of a current serial only a few hours after she was born, I am not surprised that she 'imbibed' a flair for writing. She was literally nursed to the click of the typewriter keys.

Pat was no small 'Dresden-china baby' like her golden-haired sister, Eve. She weighed nearly nine pounds; was red in the face, had a thatch of black hair (which rapidly came off), and even at that age, enormous blue eyes with long lashes. She still has them. She was a lusty baby with a fine show of spirit. Right from the start she seemed to have a sense of humour. She ought to have been a boy. As she grew older she exhibited a liking for boyish games—climbing trees, exploring, any kind of sport. She developed a keen intelligence, an imagination *and* a hot temper. She and I clashed furiously on many occasions! But she was a splendid, courageous little girl with lots of personality, and could be extremely amusing.

Today she, herself, is the hard-working author of over fifty novels and several children's books.

Each time I expected a child I had prepared the name 'Henry' for 'him'—after my husband's famous uncle. Each time *Henry* had to be forgotten!

What might so easily have been a fatal accident befell poor little Pat when she was only three months' old.

I had taken her with Eve by train down to Essex to see their grandfather who was always interested in what he called 'the little mites'. We returned home by the Brighton Belle. I ordered tea. Pat lay on my lap and cooed which she was very good at doing—she was a contented baby. I took off her bonnet. Eve sat beside me flipping through a picture-book. A middle-aged woman sitting opposite us had also ordered tea. Her tray arrived first. A man on the other side of the car got up suddenly to remove his coat, jerked the tray out of the waiter's hands with his elbow, and all the boiling water in the jug poured over Pat's face and head.

For one paralysing moment I thought this would kill her.

Everybody in the car stood up and gathered around us deeply concerned.

Luckily the first impact of the water was upon Pat's skull rather than her face, although it poured down her cheeks and my horrified eyes watched the great blisters rise on the little pink face and downy head.

The waiter, pale and shaking, rushed to find a tube of anti-burn cream which he said the engine driver was sure to have (it was in 1921 that this happened, and the Brighton trains were still being driven by steam).

Pat let out a piercing scream which at least showed me that she was alive. The waiter returned with the cream and I covered her face and head with it and put a handkerchief over her head. I have never felt more anguished.

One sideline on human nature is worth recording, just because it seems to unbelievable. The good lady who had been sitting opposite us and who had kept a deadly silence during the accident, suddenly rapped her table and said in a loud angry voice:

'Waiter! May I ask *when* you are going to bring me my tea?'

By the time I had recovered sufficiently to be able to attend to Eve, the two-year-old, the train was long past Redhill. Dear Eve was missing. She was discovered under the table, holding a bowl of sugar which had dropped from the tray, solemnly eating one lump after the other.

I was in tears for the rest of the journey. As soon as we reached Brighton I took the children by taxi to the Alexandra Hospital. There in the Out-Patients they dressed my poor baby's injuries and upon feeling her pulse, remarked with surprise that it was quite normal. She had not been too badly affected by the burns. But on her head to this day, there are two round white scars which she bears as a souvenir of the horrid episode.

5

WE settled (what we called 'permanently') in Brighton. I was becoming a well-known romantic novelist and making more money, so could afford a nicer house.

Arthur made a slow but steady financial recovery. He began to do well on the Baltic. He joined forces with two other grain brokers and became junior partner of the new firm. It prospered. We were soon what is called 'comfortably off'.

In 1924, Hodder and Stoughton published my first novel, which was called *Sealed Lips*.

In 1926 we had the General Strike. I went to Hove Town Hall where they had set up an emergency centre, and worked as a sort of 'distiller of news'. We had only earphones to bring us radio news in those days—no loud speakers. Because I could type at such a rate, I was able to take down the announcements as they came through from hour to hour. Then I distributed copies to the various departments. I hope never again to witness a strike like that one. Industry was totally hit. Trains, buses, the underground, the trams, the factories came to a standstill.

I remember a disagreeable moment when I drove down East Street in my car bearing a banner with the words 'LIFTS TO WORKERS'. When I was not in the Town Hall, I used to try and pick up those who were loyal to their jobs walking wearily to and from their offices. Suddenly I saw a surging crowd of strikers coming down East Street towards me. They surrounded the car—I had to brake pretty sharply—one man jumped on the running board, tore off the banner and trampled on it. Several shouted at me:

'You're on the wrong side, Miss!'

They looked rather ugly for a moment. I can't say I ever want to repeat the episode; but after a moment they showed some good-humour, and finally made a passage for me and let me drive on. I am not likely to forget the General Strike.

During the 'twenties I came across another famous family—

the Pertwees. Possibly of all my friends, Roland Pertwee, author and dramatist, made the greatest impact on my life and work.

I met him just before Pat was born. He and I had mutual friends; Geoffrey Colbourne—a Brighton solicitor, and his wife, Dorothy, with whom I had worked during the war. They had a son, Michael—a clever boy who became a doctor and is now a Professor of Tropical Medicine.

One evening I went to see a charity performance of a play which was produced on the West Pier in aid of the Blind Babies Home. Roland played lead.

I remember being struck by his good looks. He was a tall, golden-haired, fresh-complexioned man with bright, penetrating eyes, a handsome profile and scintillating wit.

He had once been on the stage as a professional actor and in his youth played with Henry Irving. He knew more about Shakespeare's plays than anyone I had ever met. He could quote, with astonishing memory, from almost any poet one mentioned, and he could paint. He had also studied art in Paris.

Dorothy Colbourne, petite, attractive and amusing, was playing 'opposite' him in this show on the Pier. It was an amateur show but Roland lifted it to professional heights.

I was by then a frequent visitor at the Colbournes' home. I soon saw a lot more of Roland Pertwee. He had just divorced his first wife. His two sons, Michael and John (later to be known as Jon, the famous comedian) were being brought up by their grandmother. I soon found out that any time spent in Roland's company was certain to be interesting and amusing. So there began a friendship between us that lasted for nearly forty years.

Roland took an interest in my work. He was good for me as nobody else had ever been because he was a ruthless critic and did not hesitate to be brutally frank. He would not allow me to be over-sentimental or too 'sugar-sweet'. Often he would take a blue pencil and with merciless precision slash a few paragraphs or haul me over the coals for careless writing. He, himself, was a master of the art—never a superfluous word could be found in any of his superb short stories. I was too verbose and extravagant. (After all I had been brought up on Ouida, and profligate though she was with words, and her glowing chimerical descriptions of people and places, she had no great literary quality. She was just a romantic writer in the most sentimental meaning of the word.)

Roland wanted me to be more restrained, for which I am eternally grateful. He also taught me to laugh at myself. From him I learned that unless one can laugh at oneself, one has no hope of being taken seriously (if that is not too much of a paradox!).

At first I was afraid of such ruthless criticism. But soon I grew deeply attached to Roland. Ours was an association which remained platonic and was never spoiled by 'sex'.

The Griffith family came into my life shortly after Arthur and I lived in Brighton. John was a distinguished surgeon at the Sussex County Hospital. Maud, his wife, an equally distinguished gynaecologist, was a handsome, vital woman with a wonderful nature. They became close friends of mine.

I was godmother to their second son, Adrian, of whom I shall have more to say later in this book.

In 1924 when Arthur and I moved to a flat also in Adelaide Crescent he was able to afford some shooting under the shadow of the Downs near Fulking. He organised a syndicate which consisted of himself, Roland, Aubrey Eels, a charming officer in the Gunners stationed then in Brighton, and John Griffith. I shall never forget those shooting parties—the excitement and the anticipation as the first day of September approached every year.

At these times, Arthur was at his best. That is how I like to remember him. I can still see his tall lean figure in tweed sports-coat with worn leather elbows, his gaiters, his fair head gleaming in the sun, gun raised to one shoulder; the gallant way he limped for miles over the stubbled fields. He was a fine shot. He used a 16-bore because since he was wounded in the war it tired him to carry a heavier gun. He could get a difficult woodcock or snipe with ease. He was in his element when he was organising a shoot and always on splendid terms with the other men.

He liked to sit in some big quiet barn happily entertaining the friends who shot with him. Maud Griffith or I generally took a picnic lunch down to the men. Joints of beef, crisp loaves of bread, cheeses and crates of beer. It was great fun.

Arthur was knowledgeable about the birds, the lie of the land, the whole sport. His two black Labradors, Phyl and Jem, were always at his heels. Hutchings, his gamekeeper, was an able man who reared the young birds and organised the beaters.

I shall always remember the pair of magnificent golden pheasants which Arthur bought and kept in a cage on show near the keeper's cottage.

One ghastly night a fox got in and bit off the heads of both these showbirds. Everybody was upset but we tried to be practical and not waste the two plump pheasants; so they were cooked for dinner. It was such a melancholy meal, we could hardly bear to eat it; especially when Arthur gloomily remarked while carving (which he always did extremely well) that we were about to eat £25 worth of dinner!

Another of our 'shooting friends' was Sir Patrick Hastings, the brilliant barrister, who became Attorney-General when the Labour Government got back. Both Pat and Mary, his beautiful wife, became good friends of ours. We were delighted when they rented a house in Balcombe one whole winter.

Pat Hastings could be a difficult short-tempered man and a very cynical one; but he was encouraging about my writing.

I remember once how he looked around my home and said:

'So you've paid for all this with your brains and your typewriter—not bad for a woman!'

I remember, too, after he brilliantly defended a woman in a sensational murder case and got her off, I wrote to congratulate him. My letter ended:

'If I ever commit a murder I hope you'll defend me, dear Pat.'

His reply was typical:

'Dear Denise,

If you ever commit a murder I am sure you'll be quite capable of defending yourself.

Yours, Pat.'

6

My third daughter Anne, was born on the 12th August, 1927. She was another blue-eyed, fair-haired Robins and a fine baby. It seemed obvious to me by then that I would not produce the son I wanted so much. I was very ill after Anne's birth and took longer to recover than with the other two.

Anne turned out to be my musical one; even when she was a tiny girl she could sing in tune and copy almost any melody that she heard on her nursery gramophone. She looked a little like Eve but was very different in character. She was a studious rather solitary child. It always amused me when I invited another little girl to play with her. I would go out, return later, and find each of them playing alone at opposite ends of the garden. Anne was not at that age a 'mixer'. She was particularly fond of Pat who was so clever at 'Let's Pretend', organising games and making things. As small children they were inseparable.

I asked Geoffrey Colbourne to be Anne's godfather but unfortunately he did not live to know her. He died at the very young age of thirty-six soon after Anne's christening.

When Anne was two, Arthur and I decided that as we were able to afford a good staff, flat life in Hove threatened to become too cramped. In addition we believed it to be the best for the three children that we should move into the country. We found a little house called 'Nether Birch' near the Birch Hotel in Haywards Heath. I got the builders to erect a wooden hut in the garden. I used this as a study. It was the first real one that I could call my own and where I could work in peace.

The two elder girls now went to day school, beginning with

114

the convent in Haywards Heath and going on to the P.N.E.U. school in Burgess Hill. For little Anne I found a nursery governess. In this capacity, Joan Ashworth arrived on the scene. She was a fair, charming girl, dedicated to her work. She remained with us for ten long years, becoming, with time, a close friend of the Robins' family.

We had a car. We all went down to Devonshire or Cornwall, or abroad, for the school holidays. And all the time I kept on writing, writing, writing—never allowing even illness to keep me from my typewriter.

My output soared and because of that my name became more widely known.

Still, I was not happy. Looking back I can see how restless I must have been, always searching, consciously or unconsciously for the romantic love which escaped me.

I was confident then, and still am, that the only thing a woman truly needs is to love and to be loved, and that nothing can be emptier than the golden bowl of success.

It was sad that Arthur and I could not get on, because fundamentally we respected one another. We both began to live only for our children and our separate careers.

It was while we were at 'Nether Birch' that Anne, then about three years old, escaped on to the main road and was knocked down by a cyclist and brought in with an ugly cut right across her forehead. At the time Arthur and I had just driven off to visit our friends, the Harveys, who had been posted to Bulford Camp. After covering that eighty miles we stepped into the Harveys' house only to be told that the news of this accident had just been telephoned through, whereupon we turned round, stepped back into the car, and drove home as fast as we dared go. The two local doctors, Mather and Dodd, had been summoned, laid poor little Anne on the kitchen table and stitched her up. Apparently she suffered this operation without anesthetic and with the utmost courage, screaming each time the needle went in, then asking them, smiling, what they were going to do next. Anne always showed an interest in surgery!

It is lucky that the jagged wound was so close to the hairline. The scar is there to this day.

For a short time I owned a flat in Whitehall Court (my birthplace). There I had one brief amusing encounter with the great master of words—Bernard Shaw.

I knew that he had a flat on the floor below mine. From afar I used often to catch a glimpse of the lean familiar figure wearing his knicker-bocker suit and flat cap. With the fervour of youth and a reverence for great brains that I always felt, I worshipped Mr. Shaw. I used to feel (rather childishly, perhaps), that if one day I could just go up in the lift alone with him it would be a privilege!

That day came.

I found myself alone in that very lift with *him*. As we ascended slowly I cast enraptured side-glances at Shaw's white-bearded face. From under their bushy brows his twinkling eyes turned towards me for a second then glanced away with an indifference which cut me to the quick.

Just before we reached his floor, in a silly schoolgirl manner I broke out:

'Oh, Mr. *Shaw* if only this lift would go on for ever!'

He turned to me looking astonished.

'What on earth for?' he demanded.

'You could teach me so much!' I stammered.

The lift stopped. Shaw got out. He clanged the iron gate across, thrust a bony finger through and pointed at me:

'Young woman,' he snapped, 'I couldn't teach *you* anything,' and he vanished down the corridor.

Abashed, I went up to my own flat. At the time I didn't find what he said nearly as funny as I do now. However, a few minutes later, a page-boy rang my front door bell. He said:

'Mr. Shaw's compliments, madam, but when he spoke to you he didn't know 'oo you were!'

So, at least, the great Shaw had acknowledged the fact that I was worth an apology. I could have kissed the little page. I felt considerably better.

I had the thrill, too, of meeting Somerset Maugham at a literary party.

At that time he was in his sixties. He was talking to another man when I first saw him. For a moment I watched him. I was struck by the extraordinary concentration on his face, and the brightness of those penetrating eyes on that fascinating, lined face.

To me, he has always been one of the greatest short story-tellers of our time. I found somebody to introduce me to him. He talked to me about his recent visit to the South Seas. In his witty way he described how one morning he had walked into an empty bungalow and found two little native boys scraping the paint off a door.

'I s-s-stopped them and g-g-g-gave them some money,' he stuttered, 'then b-b-b-bought the door from the owner who hadn't the least idea what the boys had been t-t-t-trying to d-d-destroy.'

'What was it?' I asked.

He lifted a sardonic eyebrow and smiled at me.

'A G-G-G-Gauguin,' he said, and added that he had had the whole door shipped back to England.

I must say that amused me. It's a good short story in itself.

I tried to persuade Arthur to live in Whitehall Court with me but nothing would induce him to do so. So I returned to the country.

By now, Roland was married to Dorothy Colbourne—Geoffrey's widow. They had bought a huge Victorian basement house in Drayton Gardens which they furnished in great taste. It became the centre of entertainment among all the friends in our circle.

Through the years that followed Arthur and I were guests at many unique parties there, and there I met painters, writers, actors, etc., so many of whom were destined to wear the laurels of fame.

In those days amateur theatricals were popular. Such shows given by Roland and myself became regular affairs and were much in demand by our friends. Roland and I actually invented the dialogue as we went along. I always flung myself whole-heartedly into these shows and with Roland as both actor and producer we couldn't go far wrong. Some of our shows were better than many professional plays. There was plenty of talent in our set. Noel Streatfeild, then just starting her own career as a writer, loved to act in our shows. What wonderful children's stories she writes today!

Roland once gave a Christmas party that I shall remember. Laurence Olivier, who at that time was married to Roland's cousin, Jill Esmond Moore, was a guest, also Patrick Hastings and his wife and the Claude Hulberts.

During the evening, Roland organised charades. Larry Olivier was then only a boy. I remember being so impressed by his looks—his dark handsome eyes—his wonderful voice. Even then a special aura of glamour surrounded him. It amuses me now to remember that once I actually acted with him—positively the first and last time I was ever to 'play opposite' the man who became England's greatest actor.

Those evening entertainments probably sound childish to the young today, but we thought them wonderful. They will never be repeated. There are no charades in this era. Gone, too, are the days when people recited, as Roland once did, and held us all spellbound.

He had a fabulous repertoire. He and I went into a kind of partnership in which I provided the incidental music on the piano, while he spoke his lines. My children say they have never forgotten his highly dramatic rendering of *The Green Eye of The Little Yellow God*, or how we all wept over his poignant rendering of *Beautiful Evelyn Hope Is Dead*.

Roland could make us either laugh or cry.

Certainly he could be immensely funny and he had a scintillating wit which he could use either to amuse—or at times, scarify!

I remember him once taking me to a play which he very much wanted to see. During the first act, two women seated immediately in front of us whispered and giggled to each other incessantly.

Roland was maddened. At last, unable to contain himself a moment longer he tapped each one on the shoulder. They turned round. Roland leaned forward and said in a grave voice:

'Pardon me, but they are making such a hell of a row on the

118

stage, I can't hear one *word* you two are saying!'

They were reduced to stupefied silence.

The years rushed by. The time was to come when the Second World War divided us—broke up our old association and many of the old familiar ties. But to me those days held a glamour that is missing now.

Never shall I forget when Roland took a house in Dulverton, a beautiful place perched high on a hill overlooking the winding silver ribbon of the Exe and the deep green Devon valley. There, he and Dorothy used to fish for trout and salmon, and there the boys of the two families spent their holidays—Michael Colbourne whom we called 'Coby', and the two Pertwees.

Michael Pertwee was destined to become a famous film and television writer, and the author of so many successful plays for Brian Rix. Jon is equally well known as a comedian and actor, now famous on television as 'Doctor Who'.

Arthur and I were Roland's guest at the First Night of *Interference*, in which he collaborated with Harold Deardon. It was a terrific success. Gerald du Maurier played lead. Herbert Marshall suddenly leapt into fame in that play. Not long afterwards he married Edna Best. Frank Lawton was in the cast as a lift boy and for him, too, the gateway to fame suddenly opened.

Arthur and I were also invited to the supper party given by the two authors after the play at the Garrick Club. It was unforgettable for me. I was seated between two of the most distinguished men of the day—Gerald du Maurier and Patrick Hastings—each in turn to receive a knighthood.

With awe, I listened to the brilliant repartee that flashed around the table between these great men.

Then, three years later, I went to a First Night in which I had a more personal interest. The night of the 15th October, 1929, at the St. James's Theatre, when a play entitled *Heat Wave* was produced; a play in which I myself collaborated with Roland.

For some time he had been interested in the story which I originally wrote for a magazine. A well-known American

119

producer of the time. Walter Hackett, produced the play. Herbert Marshall was chosen as leading man, with Phyllis Neilson-Terry playing opposite him. And in that same play Ann Todd had her first big part as a *jeune fille*.

It was a stimulating experience for me. I took a small furnished flat in Victoria and stayed there while the play went into rehearsal. I used to walk across St. James's Park every morning to the theatre, feeling gloriously happy and full of hope that *Heat Wave* was going to be as big a success as *Interference*. But, Roland, ever a restraining influence, was not so sure. He was more experienced. He knew what heart-aches and disappointments there could be in the theatrical profession for actors and playwrights alike.

Nothing, however, damped my enthusiasm and my family shared in it. It was all a great change from turning out romantic serials.

We were due to open in Cardiff—then in London at the St. James's Theatre. Walter Hackett was a vigorous producer. Roland, as good at production as he was at writing, put in his say. I was in heaven. For a time all my personal woes were forgotten. I was absorbed in the play and could think of nothing else.

Heat Wave was a roaring success right from the opening night in Cardiff. Various defects were put right up there. Roland, who rarely made prophecies of the kind, announced that we were in for a good time in London. The provincial reviews had been so encouraging.

There was only one bad moment during that First Night. The revolver which Bart Marshall was supposed to fire jammed. He clicked it madly. Nothing happened. I could see Roland, who was standing beside me in the wings, turning quite pale. Without the sound of that shot the drama would be ruined. Then with great presence of mind he clapped his big strong hands together and made a resounding imitation of a revolver shot. Although it was not the real thing, at least it saved the day. The 'wounded' actor fell to the floor. The curtain came down and the audience cheered.

Roland put a hand to his sweating forehead and cursed the

Props Manager who had failed to have a second automatic ready. I may say from that night onward there was always a reserve.

Our First Night in London—15th October, 1929, at the St. James's Theatre, was my biggest thrill.

I sat in the author's box beside Roland, wearing a black velvet dress 'by Molyneux'. That particular smell which one always associates with the stage rose to my nostrils like the sweetest incense as the curtain went up. I was nervous. We all were, but Bart Marshall played magnificently. Phyllis Neilson-Terry had never looked more beautiful, and endowed her part with all the fire and talent she inherited from her famous parents.

On the programme I saw the printed words *'Heat Wave' by Roland Pertwee from a story by Denise Robins*. I felt so proud.

When the final curtain fell, Roland appeared on the stage to make a speech—at the end of it he waved a hand in my direction and implied that he owed much to my original story. The audience turned to the box and clapped for me. It was intoxicating. A tremendous moment in my life. I was feverishly excited. The supper party that followed on the stage with the whole cast was also unforgettable.

Next morning, St. John Ervine, one of the finest reviewers of his day, openly prophesied in the *Sunday Times* that *Heat Wave* would run for three years. Roland thought he had the biggest success on his hands since *Interference*. I could see myself becoming famous in a line other than romance.

But the reviewers were all rather exaggerated. The play ran—but only for three months in London. After which it toured for two years in the provinces. Both Roland and I made money but not as much as we had anticipated. Yet when we woke that morning after the First Night and read the newspapers we had every right to be optimistic.

'Good steady entertainment'—The Times
'Instant and huge success'—The Morning Post
'Good strong theatrical plot'—Daily Telegraph

'Interesting—full of telling situations'—Daily Mail
'Swift-moving scenes of excitement and emotion'—Evening Star
'Should run indefinitely'—Daily Herald

What more could an author desire? Praise was lavished on the scenery which had been painted by young Laurence Irving. He was a gifted artist but destined, alas, to be drowned at sea. He went down in *The Empress of Ireland* not long after our play was produced.

Heat Wave was eventually put on in New York. Basil Rathbone played Herbert Marshall's part; but it was not as successful there as in London. Finally a film was made with William Powell in the lead.

It was quite a blow to Roland and myself when the London run ended but I was assured that even three months at St. James's could be counted as good. However, Roland had been right. You just mustn't count your chickens in the theatre until they are well and truly hatched.

It certainly gave me a taste for the theatre. Not long afterwards Roland and I decided to collaborate fully over another play.

It was not until 1935 that we did this; then we completed a comedy entitled *Further Outlook*. It was my original plot and this time I wrote part of the actual play.

Edna Best bought it. We went into rehearsal with Komisarjevsky—one of the most brilliant producers of his time—as director. Carol Goodner—then married to Val Gielgud—was in the cast and Ronnie Shiner appeared as a garage-mechanic. It was one of his first Cockney parts. He was an instant success.

George Sanders also suddenly appeared in all our lives. He had been recommended to Edna by Noel Coward. He had been appearing in a recent Coward Revue with success. He was tall, handsome and charming. I thought him wonderful. Unfortunately, rehearsals proved him unsuitable for that particular part. At the last moment Edna decided that Jack Hobbs should play in George's place.

122

We were staying at the Queen's Hotel in Birmingham for the opening night. The play was rapturously received. We thought we were in for another success. I was full of hope, because this was the first time I had ever been billed as the actual co-author of a play.

After the Birmingham production, however, Edna, who was charming but capricious, fell in love with yet another play that had been sent to her from Paris by the famous dramatist, Henri Bernstein. She decided that she preferred to launch the Bernstein play. So the whole thing folded up and we never reached London. It was a bitter blow. I learned how fickle fortune can be to those who write or produce plays.

One incident connected with George Sanders stands out in my memory on the First Night of *Further Outlook*.

Edna gave a supper at the Queen's Hotel for the whole cast. An awkward situation arose. Jack Hobbs was now our leading man, but George Sanders was still in the hotel. Somewhat mistakenly, Edna did not include George in our party. I was personally disappointed. I admired the witty suave Mr. Sanders.

The *Further Outlook* party all sat at one long table, drinking toasts to each other. George sat alone at his own table only a few yards away, impeccable in white tie and tails, and wearing a carnation in his buttonhole. He looked like a man with a million dollars, in solitary splendour, sipping his champagne. Never once did he glance in our direction. Finally, he got up and sauntered out as though he owned the restaurant, still not so much as glancing towards us. It was quite a magnificent gesture. He was supremely independent. When I said goodbye to George the next morning and told him how sorry I was that things had turned out this way, he kissed me, gave that sardonic smile destined to become so famous, and drawled:

'My dear, no matter! I intend to show Edna and all of them one day that they have made a great mistake about me.'

He did; and I take off my hat to him. I don't need to tell anybody what a success George was as soon as he reached Hollywood.

Now Eve and Pat went to boarding school.

Everything was going well except my personal life. Unfortunately the misunderstandings between Arthur and myself increased as we grew older. We were both miserable about it and conscious that we were failing each other, yet unable to alter the fact that we were two such utterly different people.

I am afraid that in the end we both gave up trying to find a solution to the problem. All that we then wanted was that while the children were at home they should not know that their parents were unhappy. During the holidays our lives were led entirely for them. We really did make an effort to refrain from quarrelling in front of them. In more humorous vein, these days, they tell me they remember various arguments taking place when we were all out in the car. Arthur and I always thought that we knew the best way and could never agree to the routes. I wonder how many other married couples disagree on the same basis! Anyhow, the children found these arguments quite funny.

I remember old Charles Boon, then my publisher, visiting me in Sussex one Sunday. I opened a cupboard in my study to show him a pile of manuscripts. He gave them one glance, then said:

'I'll give you a good cheque now this moment for the rights of the whole lot.' (He mentioned a tempting sum.) But my business sense had developed with the years and I laughingly refused his offer.

'You are right, you know!' said Charles with a twinkle.

What with my busy domestic life, my exacting children during the holidays, and my literary work all the year round, there was hardly a spare moment in my existence. One thing was clear to me. I had to go on travelling. Each new country I visited gave me just the inspiration for the romantic backgrounds I needed for my books.

My engagement diary was always full. I lectured, spoke at literary meetings, and went to Literary Lunches, opened Bazaars, Flower Shows, Dog Shows! What did I not do!

I took a great interest in clothes. I wrung every ounce of interest I could from Life. But I was still in love with *Love*, and that seemed to me one impossible thing to find; Ivor

Novello described it so aptly in one of his songs: *'Love is the reason for living'*. And I had so desperately wanted it to be mine.

7

ONE morning I woke up and realised that I was on the wrong side of thirty. I felt old and sad, and when I was introduced to a girl who recommended me a holiday in a little Andalusian village called Torremolinos, I decided to take her advice, leave my family for a month and go out to Spain.

I took Marjorie Hervey, my secretary from Haywards Heath, with me. I decided to write a Spanish romance. We took rooms in a Moorish castle known as *'Santa Clara'*. Every morning I sat with Marjorie in the sunlit courtyard which they called the 'Quartel' dictating to her—both of us in swim-suits.

It was warm and beautiful and full of glamour there. I shall never forget the beauty of the dark palms against the sky at night, and the enormous glittering stars.

The gypsies used to come up from the beach to dance the Flamenco for us. Everybody drank Malaga wine while they listened to the sad raucous singing.

We went on donkey picnics, riding our little grey beasts far up into the hills and eating cold tortillos (omelettes) for lunch. Once I was induced to go to a bull fight in Malaga and feel a bit ashamed of the fact that I rather enjoyed it—but only when the horses were not present.

How could I fail to be impressed when it was the famous, one-and-only Belmonte whom I saw that day—kneeling with his back to the great panting bull, waiting until it charged, then when it was within an inch of those wicked horns, pirouetting and driving his sword straight through the aorta—to the frenzied applause of the crowd. But I wouldn't like to see a bad matador in action, and never in fact wish to see another bull fight.

Sometimes while I dictated to Marjorie Hervey, the peasants used to creep around, lie flat on their stomachs in a circle and watch and listen to us, fascinated.

My secretary and I left Gibraltar for Tangier by boat. It was on that boat that I met quite a famous character who was half-English, half-Spanish. He was a big man in the police force in Tangier. A handsome, conceited young man, he wore a resplendent uniform and rows of medals which I am sure he had bought for himself!

Daily he would walk through Tangier, saluting to the right and to the left, believing himself a kind of Mussolini, because he had strict control in that international port and it was in his hands to decide whether passports should or should not be stamped. He kept a stranglehold on the native population. They all seemed afraid of him. Down in the ship's lounge he stamped my own passport prior to our disembarking. Then— so he afterwards said—looked up at me and fell madly in love with 'the English lady writer'. He at once volunteered to show me around Tangier.

I accepted his offer and lived to regret it. From that moment onward, huge bouquets arrived twice a day at my room in the El Minza Hotel, and scores of invitations from him which I kept turning down. There were times when I quite enjoyed talking to the conceited, handsome police officer, but for the most part I found him a bore—even comic, which was the last thing he would wish. His vanity was colossal.

Rather foolishly one day I accepted his offer to show me something of the night-life of Tangier. I remember Marjorie shaking her head in horror as she saw me drive off that evening to keep the rendez-vous. She wondered if she would ever see me back alive, but I was inquisitive about things and anxious to investigate 'life-in-the-raw' in Tangier.

It was arranged that I should meet the police officer at a villa which, he said, belonged to a friend not far from my hotel. First, he must keep an important business date but he would join me as soon as possible.

I should have 'smelt a rat'. I didn't. When I arrived at the villa—I went by car—it looked curiously shuttered and deserted. I wondered if I had come to the wrong place. I foolishly dismissed my taxi and pulled a rusty old bell. Maybe, I thought, my secretary had been right and I had walked into a trap and never would see England again! Yet it was such a bewitching night—the stars were enormous—the sound of plaintive native music drifted from the Kasbah. Tangier Harbour twinkled with lights. It was a night for romance. I had come here for 'copy'. Why be silly and mistrustful? With a policeman I ought to be safe!

Still, I was on the verge of turning away and walking back to the El Minza when the front door of the villa opened. An old woman looked out cautiously. She had the appearance, I thought, of a custodian of a prison. A huge bunch of keys dangled from her leather belt. In halting Spanish, I explained to her who I had come to meet. She replied in Spanish. She seemed to know all about me. At once she invited me in. She expected me, she said.

Feeling relieved, I walked into the hall, but as she locked and bolted the big heavy door after me, I once again began to fear that I had been a little too venturesome and might have to pay a heavy price for carrying my search for romantic episode this far.

The old woman looked me up and down approvingly. She used the words I had heard before: '*Muy guapa*'. I was wearing a black chiffon evening dress with silver foxes around my shoulders, and a diamond brooch, and wristlet watch.

The old woman was gabbling nineteen to the dozen! I couldn't understand one word. Then came the shock. I was led into a room and there, seated at a long table, smoking, reading or sewing, were about a dozen girls; *all stark naked*. They wore literally nothing but high-heeled satin shoes.

Before I could recover they leapt up and surrounded me like a lot of excited schoolgirls. They jabbered in diverse tongues, mostly unrecognisable. I was relieved to hear some French, for my eyes by this time were popping out of my head! I turned to the French girl and begged her to tell me where I was and what this was all about.

She beamed at me. Like the others she was heavily made-up

127

and very attractive. They all had beautiful figures. I suppose the average ages ranged between sixteen and twenty. The French girl told me that this place was called '*La Maison Blanc*' and that it was a 'House of Joy' where they 'entertained men.' *A very expensive house*, of course, she said proudly. They considered themselves an exclusive lot.

'You, *chérie*, must be the new English girl we are expecting,' she finished gaily.

Dumbfounded I stared from her to the old custodian. Then we carried on a three-handed rather disjointed discussion most of which I did not understand, while the rest of the girls kept touching my fur, my jewellery and my dress; calling me *très chic*—and appraising my value.

It was now perfectly obvious to me what sort of place I was in. Horrified, I demanded to be let out immediately. When the old woman shook her head, I lost my temper and told the French girl to explain to *Madame* that I was a well-known English citizen and that if she did not immediately unlock the front door for me, the police officer would punish them all and the British Consul would have the 'House' closed down. I explained that I was certainly *not* 'the new girl'. They might well be expecting one, but they had made a bad mistake.

It was an unpleasant affair, exciting only in retrospect. I must say at the time I have never felt more scared. Afterwards I saw the funny side.

It wasn't long before another woman came on the scene. *She* was a surprise to me. She was English—elegantly dressed. She had a sad lovely if ravaged face and spoke in a most cultured voice. After hearing my complaint, she apologised profusely, sent the old woman about her business, and took me away from all the other chattering magpies. She offered me some champagne in a quiet, beautifully furnished *salon* on the other side of the villa. Her own private room, apparently.

She was most distressed about this, she said. The police officer was a fool ever to have arranged to meet me here. She supposed that he had wanted me to see '*La Maison Blanc*' in order that I would write about it, but he should have warned me. Unfortunately they *had* been expecting a 'new girl' from

London and old Caterina had made the mistake of thinking I was the one. She explained, also that 'La Maison Blanc' was one of a chain of such houses throughout Europe, and that the girls were often interchanged so that the gentlemen who lived in the district and came here regularly might enjoy variety!

My policeman turned up, sweating and full of profuse apologies, but he roared with laughter when he heard what had happened. He thought it an immense joke. However, by this time, I was cross and all desire to 'do the town' had left me. I demanded to be taken back to El Minza immediately.

He shrugged his shoulders, looked a bit crestfallen but did not argue. He realised he had slipped up.

The *Madame* walked to the front door with us, gave me a wistful smile and said:

'Give my love to London. I was born there but I shall never go back now. My life is here.'

I began to ask if I could do anything for her but she shook her head and smiled.

'It is too late,' she said.

I felt sad. It took me a little time to forget that woman's haunting face. The life she had chosen for herself had certainly brought *her* no happiness.

It was the first and last evening I ever spent in the company of the notorious officer. (Later I learned that he had a bad name with women, and shortly afterwards I heard that he had died.) At the time of our association I made every excuse to see no more of him. He seemed maddened by the rejection. Now, with all the fruit and flowers, there also arrived notes written by him in broken English—often screamingly funny. One began:

'*My English beloved. When I see you my heart stops and I am asphyxe . . .*'

Well, I am afraid I had no interest in 'asphyxiating' him. I blamed myself for having encouraged even a casual friendship with him. I had learned my lesson. One could not make friends with such a man.

He even sent me a first class railway ticket to Madrid. I was to travel with him and there stay as his guest, or, he wrote—he

129

would shoot me.

That ended things. Marjorie, utterly scandalised and alarmed, besought me to leave Tangier at once.

'You've got all the copy you want, and you don't want to be murdered,' she grumbled.

Poor Marjorie. I think she began to imagine that her own throat might well be slit in this city of pock-marked natives, wailing songs—*and* unscrupulous policemen.

I sat down and composed a very short, sharp letter to my troublesome admirer.

'*My husband arrives at the El Minza tonight. He is one of the best shots in England* . . .'

The ruse worked. The infatuated officer never came near me nor wrote to me again. He was a coward.

Before leaving Tangier, I felt there was one more experience I must have. I must cross the Riff Mountains and visit Ceuta. This, I decided to do alone.

I knew that my mother was taking a sea voyage for her health and travelling alone as my step-father could not get away. Her ship, *The Ubena*, was due in at Ceuta for a day, en route for Portugal. I decided to meet her.

Leaving Marjorie behind to pack up for our final departure, and type the notes I had made, I boarded the little bus for the long journey.

Just how rough it was going to be, I had no idea. I was the only European on that bus except the driver. He was a Spaniard; a villainous looking fellow with a squint and long black moustaches. He smilingly invited me to sit beside him. The rest of the passengers were a sorry collection of natives, men in dirty white or striped robes, veiled women looking like white bundled nuns, who looked at me out of their large black-kohled eyes with great curiosity.

In the seat behind me, I saw a man holding a large net filled with tiny struggling birds which he had trapped. There must have been dozens of them fluttering and gasping in the heat, for it was well over eighty-five degrees. The sun blazed down from a hard blue sky. The mountains looked fierce and sinister in the distance. I began to wonder if I had been unwise to make this journey as we rattled along, bumping and shaking. One Arab, wearing a turquoise-blue burnous, actually slept throughout the journey. I envied him.

The thought of the tiny suffocating birds caused me such pain that I finally turned to the man and asked him in my sketchy Spanish what he meant to do with them. Showing splendid teeth, he grinned and explained that he had netted them for sale in Tetuan—the halfway town to Ceuta where we would be stopping. They made delicious pies, he assured me. A great delicacy. I asked him how much he would make on the netful. He mentioned a small sum. I took it out of my purse and handed it to him. He gaped at me. 'All?' he asked unbelievingly. 'The *Senora* wishes to buy *all*?'

I nodded. He pocketed the money, staring at me, and handed me the birds. I asked my pock-marked moustachioed driver if he would pull up for a moment. With his villainous grin he nodded and complied. I got out and opened the net while the other passengers sat watching, dumbfounded.

I released that pitiful struggling mass of birds. One by one they revived in the air, and stretched their wings. With the exception of a few at the bottom of the net that had died they all rose and soared skyward. I watched them, satisfied and relieved, but the trapper screamed at me furiously. *What had I done? All his hard work wasted. Was I crazy?*

I reminded him coldly that he had got his price. He sat back, grumbling, shrugging. The others broke into excited jabbering and put their hands to their foreheads—laughing. The '*Inglese*' was mad, they said.

It was soon after I returned to England from this holiday that I was destined to meet in person the fascinating man whose romantic melodies had for a long time delighted me, and so many millions of others—Ivor Novello.

He had just made an enormous success with his 'Rat' series. The Rat being that mysterious and exciting figure of the Paris underworld whose exploitations made a popular theme for some of Ivor's best plays and films.

I first met Ivor after one of his First Nights, and immediately fell under his spell. Not only was he devastatingly handsome but one of the most charming, generous people I have ever known. Success never went to Ivor's head. He had a special affection and solicitude for actors, artists and musicians less lucky than himself.

Every one who knew Ivor loved him. When he died, still only in his fifties and at the height of his success, it was almost a national calamity. He was deeply mourned. Nobody has taken his place. I had a special tie with him for we *both* loved and believed in romance; and, as Ivor so charmingly put it to me on one occasion, if he was the King of theatrical romance —I was the Queen of the romantic book-world. He thought it might be a good idea if we collaborated and I were to write the novel of one or two of his plays.

He seemed pleased with my first effort—a book version of *The Triumph of the Rat*, and later, in 1935, I turned his successful play *Murder In Mayfair* into a novel. He wrote me this letter on the 3rd March, 1935, from his flat in Aldwych:

'Dear Denise,

Not only have I glanced through but have completely read *Murder In Mayfair*, and you really have done a swell job, as apart from the original interest of the play it is now an extremely good tale on its own account and awfully well written. Thank you ever so much for doing it.

Yours affectionately,
Ivor Novello.'

8

WHILE travelling from Milan to Monte Carlo one day, I found a first-class carriage to myself and settled down to read. At the last moment a young girl sprang into the carriage followed by a porter who piled in some expensive-looking luggage and a portable gramophone.

I thought this late-comer was one of the most beautiful creatures I had ever seen. In her early twenties, she had glorious red hair and magnificent eyes, golden and sparkling as sherry. She was beautifully dressed, with a huge bunch of Parma violets pinned to a snow-leopard coat. Pink and breathless, she smiled at me in a friendly way and introduced herself as Nola——

I told her my name, and learned that she was not getting out at Monte Carlo like myself but going on to Paris—then flying on to London. She came from Australia.

'I hope you like music,' she said, 'because I'm longing to play my records.'

At once a bond was established between us. Gladly I listened to her music, but was curious to know why every record was a Yehudi Menuhin violin solo.

'Because I adore his music and I adore him!' was Nola's frank reply.

I was further intrigued when she told me that she was engaged to be married to a big sheep farmer in her native country. She had come over to Europe expressly to follow Menuhin from country to country, and town to town, wherever he played. She was more than his 'fan'. Her passion for him and his violin amounted to idolatry.

I gathered that she was in love with him although she had never so far even met him. It was a romantic situation which obviously appealed to me, and when Nola heard who I was, and the sort of books I wrote, she became even more confidential.

She confessed that she did not think she could ever go back to Australia and marry her farmer. She had just heard Yehudi play in Milan. She was making for London now because next week he was due to give a concert at the Albert Hall.

This, I thought, was like a page out of one of my own novels. Yet it seemed sad that such a beautiful girl should spend all her time and money following the great violinist around the world if he was never to know about it—or her.

When I returned to London myself, ten days later, it was to receive a letter from Nola (she was staying at the Ritz), telling

133

me the fantastic news that she was about to be married—and to Yehudi Menuhin, himself.

Lucky girl! I thought. At least one woman in the world has achieved her heart's desire in a miraculous fashion.

Over the telephone, Nola excitedly described how she had listened to Menuhin's performance at the Albert Hall, then waited outside the stage exit for him to sign her autograph album.

He did so, raised his eyes from the book and glanced at her. I suppose her beauty bowled him right over, for he took her out to supper, learned how devoutly she loved his playing and how she had come from the other side of the world to hear and see him—and eventually married her.

I sentimentally believed that they would live happily ever afterwards. It is a sad fact that after a few years together and the birth of their two children, their marriage broke up—but I like to think that for a little while they were ecstatically happy.

Restlessly, we went on moving. It was in 1933 that I found my most perfect and beloved of all my houses—Furnace Pond Cottage in Slaugham—one of the most unspoiled villages in Sussex. Part Queen Anne, part Charles II, the long row of cottages face a beautiful pond fringed with beech-trees. It was at one time an old forge.

When I first saw it, two of the cottages which were joined, were still in primitive condition. There was no electricity, only lamplight; no central heating, no proper garden.

Sir Hugh and Lady Jackson owned it. They sold it to us because Lady Jackson wanted more land for her horses, and could not get it in Slaugham. Furnace Pond Cottage faces common on the north side and agricultural land on the south. There were no fields available. Neither Arthur nor I needed a lot of land. Furnace Pond Cottage seemed the ideal home for our family.

I was able by then to put down the deposit required, so we moved in, and this time I felt tremendous pride and pleasure because I was sure my three girls would fall in love with the place as I had done. They were, in fact, entranced by their new home when they came back from their boarding schools and saw the house for the first time. By then we had installed electricity. We had to buy a generator of course, as we were not yet 'on the grid'. We also put in central heating. The old house was too cold for my liking.

It was not long before we rented a piece of an adjoining field on which Arthur helped to make a tennis court for the children. Almost immediately a stroke of luck enabled me to add a new much-needed wing to the house. After this it seemed perfect.

The weekends at Furnace Pond began to be very interesting. Many famous people came down to stay. Phyllis Panting, editor of *Woman & Beauty* often spent the weekend with us. She was engaged to Digby Morton who was then rapidly rising to fame in haute couture. In the now famous Farm Street, Digby had turned an old stable into a smart little shop which he called '*La Chasse*'. On one side lived Gloria Swanson; on the other, Tallulah Bankhead. To '*La Chasse*' came all the prettiest actresses and debs to get the lovely and distinctive tweed suits from the young Irish designer.

I was a guest at the Digby Mortons' wedding at Caxton Hall. Phyllis was given away by the great H. G. Wells himself. Ruby M. Ayres, the novelist, lent her Rolls Royce for the occasion. Phyllis had never looked more attractive.

By that time, I was renting a small flat in Sloane Street so that I could spend a bit of time meeting my literary friends and attending lunches and various functions connected with my career. I continued to see much of my dear friend Roland Pertwee and his family. I lunched often at The Ivy with a publisher, or editor or literary agent. The Ivy was a kind of club in those days. The *Maître d'hotel*, Mario (later to become so famous at the Caprice) was a great figure and rapidly proving himself the best *restaurateur* in London.

Many famous people had regular tables at The Ivy. Looking back, I can still see Marie Tempest, with her pet dog beside her, lunching daily at her little corner table, or Ivor Novello with his friends. He would always spring up when I came in, hold out his arms to me and say '*Hullo, Denise darling!*' in that melting voice of his. My cousin, Sydney Carroll, lunched there every day. He had just bought the Ambassador Theatre and launched Vivien Leigh in *The Mask of Virtue*. Ursula Bloom used to come in with her tall Naval-Commander husband. She was very slight and fair, with big blue eyes—but behind that fragility, that Dresden china colouring, lay a shrewd clever journalistic mind.

As regards my career—for eight or nine years now, Mills & Boon had been my publishers. Suddenly a young man named Ivor Nicholson came along—a clever, charming journalist who, with the wealth of Bernard Watson to back his venture, launched a new publishing house—Ivor Nicholson & Watson. They wanted my name on their list. They tempted me with what was the biggest offer I had ever received from any literary quarter. A cheque for *one thousand pounds*, free, gratis, and for which I need do no work. It was merely for signing the contract!

I did not go behind Charles Boon's back. I told him the facts. Unfortunately he was so annoyed by this offer from Ivor Nicholson that he refused to compete and at once released me from my contract with his firm. Somewhat reluctantly I left my old publishers and became the new Nicholson & Watson 'star' author.

My first book with them, *Life And Love*, was published with a tremendous splash. Posters bearing the slogan 'Robins For Romance' appeared on London buses and in the underground. The next thing I knew was that the papers were 'starring me' too. The *Sunday Dispatch* published an article in which my photograph appeared between Noel Coward's and Arnold Bennett's, with the caption: *The Big Money-Makers in the Writing World*. I was entranced to be in such good company. I began to write articles for most of the leading national newspapers. I'd like to quote a few reviews of my novels which I had in those days, and hope my vanity will be forgiven for putting them on record. The papers do not go to so much trouble over romantic novelists today.

The *Daily Sketch* said: '*Few people have achieved their childhood ambitions in such a satisfactory manner as Denise Robins.*'

The *Sunday Dispatch* said: '*What a good story-teller Denise Robins is.*' Several reviews quoted my new publishers' words which headed their announcement: '*Denise Robins is the darling of England's novel-reading public.*' *The Observer* quoting this, added: '*Neither her photograph nor her style of writing would lead me to doubt that for a moment.*'

I was often called Ethel Dell's successor. James Agate, the great book critic, wrote amusing articles about several of my new novels. One of them ended with the words: '*will our readers like this? ... of course they will ... elementary, my dear Watson!*'

I suppose that this should all have made me absolutely happy. I can only say, honestly, that it did not. It only made me feel proud and thankful that the long years of hard work were paying off and that I could buy my family extra luxuries and send them to the expensive schools abroad which I felt to be necessary for their education, but which their father could do nothing about (neither did he ever believe a first-class education necessary for girls).

But I remained fantastically lonely 'in the crowd'. I used often to quote Dowson's poignant words:

When the feast is finished and the lamps expire
Then falls thy shadow, Cynara
And the night is thine ...

But who was my Cynara? What male counterpart had ever cast *his* shadow across the light of my fame and fortune? I had no idea. Only once or twice, I imagined, I had found the right man—then the dream faded again. So I went on pouring my heart out into my books but that heart remained bitterly unsatisfied.

All my friendships have sweetened my life. Best of all, Time—the greatest of all healers—gradually wiped out the animosity between my mother and myself.

She and her husband still lived in their flat in Hove. I took my young family to tea with her there regularly. They found her sweet and easy to get on with and much admired her astonishing youth. She just refused to grow old.

When she was seventy she became very interested in

137

horses and racing. She hadn't much money but enjoyed placing her small bets on the horses of her choice during the season. Her little gambles were her chief delight. In fact, till the end of her days. Mother also 'did' the football pools and was amazingly good at this. She won several small amounts. She was a living example of the fact that there is nothing like an interest no matter what—to keep a person young and vigorous—in mind if not in body.

As I approached my forties, I think my mother, alone, realised the sadness that lay under the glittering crust of my own life. We grew much closer. I could talk to her like a friend. It troubled her to realise that I had married the wrong man and that I found it hard to resign myself to the lack of love—that complete absence of romance except in my books, which took all the joy out of life for me.

My three daughters and their welfare were of paramount importance to me. I never spent a school holiday apart from them.

9

1938 dawned for me as one of the most important and fateful years of my personal life.

I began to be afraid that the girls who were growing up fast would begin to notice the incompatibility of their parents and suffer through it. The one thing I had always passionately desired was to preserve the unity of our home for them. For eighteen years Arthur and I between us had managed this. Up to then they had been happy. But I could see failure ahead now that they were adolescent. It scared me.

I was finding it increasingly difficult to conceal my emotional frustration. It must have been difficult for Arthur, too.

In early March I fell ill and went out to Egypt to convalesce as the guest of Bertie and Nancy Wiseman who were old friends of mine. Bertie was a Major in the Royal Signals.

Nancy often wrote about the good life in Cairo and wanted me to have a few weeks there in the sunshine.

I did not like going so far from the girls, but I was so nervously exhausted that my doctor advised a complete break from the domestic routine and the strain of the present situation at home. Things had got on top of me.

What happened once I reached Egypt might seem like a chapter from one of my own novels.

I spent a month in Cairo and benefited by the change and the sunshine. It was my first introduction to the Middle East. I found everything interesting, although it had no great appeal for me. I was taken to explore the Tombs of the Kings in Luxor, saw the wonders of Tutankhamen's treasures in the Cairo Museum, went for picnics in the desert, visited the Pyramids and enjoyed the splendour of those sensational sunsets on the Nile. But I thoroughly disliked the filth and corruption that lay under the so-called glamour of Egypt, just as it used to in Morocco. However, it was a fresh experience. I found plenty of 'copy' and was anxious to get home and start a new book, and *very* anxious to see my daughters again.

But fate had more than this in store for me.

Came the last day but one before I was due to leave Egypt (I had booked a passage on that crack Italian liner *The Marco Polo* which was sailing from Alexandria to Venice). I wanted to make the rest of the journey overland and meet my friends the Grahams in Monte Carlo.

(*The Marco Polo*, incidentally, was sunk during the war. I felt sorry. She was such a glorious ship.)

The Wisemans had arranged to take me to a cocktail party in a friend's flat. I was not enthusiastic as I don't drink, and I never have really enjoyed those sort of parties. They still seem a senseless waste of time to me. I like to talk to people and hear what they have to say.

Nancy persuaded me to go.

'There'll be some nice young men there, do come and add to the glamour for them,' she said.

So I went. I remember exactly what I wore. A dark grey dress and jacket made for me by my friend, Digby Morton,

139

and a big black hat. In those days my hair was still chestnut with a few strands of silver over the ear. I had noted these grey hairs with some misgiving but felt no desire to disguise them.

I went to that party without the least premonition that I was going to meet the man who would change the whole of my life.

A crowd had gathered in the beautiful flat overlooking the Nile where Mary and Norman Tate were living. Norman, like Bertie, was in the Signals. The drawing-room was full of officers. Among them I found a friend from home, Archie Montgomery-Campbell. We had mutual friends in Brighton— the Bethells. We talked about them for a few moments then suddenly I saw *him*.

He was young, quite absurdly handsome and seemed to be enjoying a joke. He was laughing. He held a glass of champagne in one hand and a cigarette in the other. He looked at me. I asked Archie his name.

'Oh, that's "Bottle" Pearson,' said Archie.

'Bottle'. The nickname they gave Neill while he was soldiering in Egypt because he used to hold such wonderful champagne parties and was always good fun.

'Introduce me,' I said to Archie. I was vastly intrigued by 'Bottle' Pearson's appearance.

A moment later he and I were talking. I learned that his name was O'Neill Pearson; that he was a Lieutenant in the R.A.S.C.; and that, of all things in the world, his mother actually lived in Haywards Heath—only six miles away from my own home; yet we had to come all these thousands of miles in order to meet! It was fate.

I didn't know then what this would all mean to me—only that I found Neill Pearson utterly charming and that he seemed to be equally intrigued with me.

'You're the woman novelist, aren't you?' he said, 'Mary Tate told me about you. I must read one of your books.'

I sent him several.

He never read one. He never *has* read one yet!

He was not the type to enjoy novels; not at all 'the literary type' I had imagined my man of destiny might be. But in

Cairo that evening I learned that there is no criterion as to what sort of man can attract a woman and hold her heart for ever. It is just that a peculiar chemistry between two people can react quite inexplicably and suddenly create an imperishable fire.

Neill and I talked and talked. I told him a bit about myself. He in turn told me that he had been born and brought up in the Lake District. His old home was in Cartmel, a beautiful little village near Windermere. His father, now dead, had been a well-known Ulverston solicitor. He had two brothers, Pat and Jack. Pat, too, was in the legal profession. Jack was still at Cambridge. They had all come south to live after their father died.

Neill was an Old Salopian. He afterwards took a degree in engineering at Peterhouse, Cambridge. (I discovered later that he had won the sculls for Peterhouse and was a fine rowing man—an all-round good sportsman.) First-class on a horse, he had also won several cups at Army point-to-points. He explained to me that he had chosen to go into the Army rather than take up civil engineering.

He was ten years younger than myself.

I could write much about our first meeting and the somewhat feverish evening we spent dining together in the 'Kit-Kat' Club on the banks of the Nile. We danced and talked for hours and somehow I felt closer to him in a few minutes than I had ever been to any other man. Before dawn broke—when we were still dancing—we realised that we were hopelessly in love.

10

I FELT rather as though the earth was being cut away from under my feet and that I was falling into a bottomless pit. I could see danger ahead. I had wanted this romance and longed for love, but I was married and I did not want happiness at anybody else's expense. In any case Neill was too young for me. His widowed mother would certainly not approve of her son becoming involved with me. There was absolutely everything against our growing too fond of each other.

We decided that we must not meet again.

I had only one day left in Cairo. It seemed to me sad and ironic that I should have met Neill only at the very end of my holiday, but my husband and children were waiting for me in England. I knew that I must put this affair right out of my life.

I fell from the heights to the depths. I let Neill drive me in his old Bentley car across the desert to Alexandria. He saw me off on *The Marco Polo*. It just seemed that we had met twenty years too late.

I remember how I stood waving to Neill—watching his figure grow smaller and smaller on the quayside as *The Marco Polo* moved out. I thought, what a *damnable* thing to have happened; what a pity really that I had ever met him. It was going to hurt—badly. It was only a strong sense of duty that drove me away from Cairo. I was certain, too, that things would be a lot less agreeable between my husband and myself and it would cost me a lot to conceal my true feelings.

I remember how a Belgian—a millionaire who owned most of Heliopolis and was travelling on the same ship as myself—saw me standing there on deck, with the tears pouring down my cheeks. He was a great one with women. He decided (so he told me) that I might make an attractive companion for the voyage. In French, he introduced himself and asked my why I was crying.

I told him frankly that it was because I was leaving the man I loved.

He gave a cynical smile and shrugged.

'*Oubliez*,' he said. 'There is always another love, *ma chère enfant*,' and pointed to himself.

I turned away. I went down to my cabin and stayed there most of the voyage. By the time we reached Venice I was in a 'state' and could think of little but Neill.

Once home, I was overjoyed to see my daughters again but found it exceedingly difficult to pick up the threads of the old routine. I was very restless and miserable. I tried to tire myself out by writing all day but everything seemed to be collapsing around me. I told Arthur what had happened and now we faced the unhappy truth. Our marriage was finished. We had to agree upon that. Fortunately, Eve and Pat were busy with their own lives; Anne was still at boarding-school. They didn't seem to need me much. That dreadful feeling of loneliness in the crowd weighed me down even more heavily than before.

Then Neill returned on leave to England—and such is the frailty of human nature—we did meet again. His home was only six miles away from mine. It was too near.

I intend to draw a blank over the months that followed. There are some things that are too private and personal to make public. Sufficient to say that I made a desperate effort to put Neill out of my life again. Not once but many times I sent him away; without success.

Arthur and I would never again see eye to eye. It was a stalemate. We were both deeply distressed but there seemed no hope of patching up our differences. The gap between us had grown too wide.

I decided that it might help if I got a really long way away and went abroad with Eve who was at an age to be companionable as well as sympathetic. By now she was understanding of the differences which existed between her parents.

We arrived in Paris. I walked into a travel agent's and asked them where we could go for a week or two. They suggested Czechoslovakia or Hungary. I chose the former. So Eve and I boarded the train that next night. We undressed and settled down in our first-class sleeper.

It seemed that the agency had slipped up. They failed to make sure that our passports were in order. We were stopped at the Customs once we crossed the border into Germany. We had no German visa.

A little man, the attendant of the sleeping car, knocked on the door of our compartment and woke us up. He looked scared.

'You must dress and pack your bags and get out at once, *Madame, Ma'moiselle. La Police!*' he said in a hoarse voice.

Mystified, we did as he said and stepped out on to the platform with our bags.

It was in early September and cold at one a.m. in the morning. Suddenly on either side of us appeared two tall young men in black uniforms. Grim and unsmiling they piloted us into an office. They carried loaded revolvers. They were the first German Stormtroopers we had ever seen (or, fortunately, ever met again!).

Now we found ourselves in a scene that has since been enacted many times on film or television. It was so typical. The bright lights, the big desk, the sinister-looking man with shaven head and strong glasses sitting behind that desk, fixing us with eyes full of suspicion. Behind him hung a full-length illuminated portrait of Hitler.

Eve and I had had no inkling that we lacked a German visa and we were nonplussed by the threatening atmosphere. I can't say, however, that we were at all frightened. As yet, the black shadow of the Swastika had not fallen across our country. The news of the Anschluss had for us been only—news. Besides, we had nothing to be afraid of. The little man fired questions at us. Why had we no visas? Where were we going? What was the purpose of our visit? Why?—why?—*why?*

We had to turn out our cases. Everything was meticulously searched. We soon realised that we were suspected of being spies. We knew of course that Runciman was in Prague trying to save the situation there, but nobody suspected that Hitler was about to march into Czechoslovakia.

In the end, Eve and I seemed able to convince our inquisitor that we were only innocent tourists. He issued temporary visas for us and ordered us sternly to go to the German Embassy the moment we reached Prague and get our passports correctly stamped.

The tall Stormtroopers were by this time relaxing and taking a second look at my beautiful Eve. I, without any inhibitions, waved a hand at the portrait of Hitler and said:

'A fine likeness!'

Eve rather nervously whispered to me to keep quiet, but the passport officer was by this time quite friendly.

'That is our great Leader,' he said proudly, lifted an arm solemnly in the direction of the painting and said: 'Heil Hitler.'

The Stormtroopers respectfully echoed the words.

I, however, was by now thoroughly disinterested in Hitler. I was thinking of those two first-class sleepers for which I had paid, and that had gone on to the next stop—Vienna—without us.

Grumbling and cold, we eventually boarded a German train which was bound for Vienna. At about four o'clock in the morning we came to a halt. A porter told us that the Paris sleeping-car train was in the way and our train had to be shunted. Suddenly Eve and I realised that this was *our* former train. We sprang out of the German Express and rushed from one into the other. Sure enough, our little sleeping-car attendant met us in the corridor and almost wept with joy. He admitted that he had never expected to see us again. So we undressed once more and slept the night through to Vienna.

After this adventure we finally got to Prague. For a week we explored the beauty and wonder of the buildings, the river and the bridges, all the glory that belonged to poor Czechoslovakia before the war. We also took a trip to Brno to see the fantastic stalactite caves. A week later we travelled home through Venice—Eve's first visit there which she found thrilling.

But for me it was one long journey of sorrow and anxiety. The future looked black. I could not enjoy myself. But we had to go home. It appeared even more hopeless, so I shut up my beautiful home and took a furnished house in Eaton Terrace. It was decorated by Oliver Messel and belonged to his sister, the Countess of Rosse.

Arthur and the girls settled in town with me for the autumn. I tried once more to save this marriage, hoping that an entirely new house and atmosphere might help. I went out a lot, and wrote as hard as ever. Life in London was a change for us all. Pat was enjoying her job at the Amalgamated Press and Eve was busy going out with her friends and admirers.

My friends rallied round—conscious now that the Robins' marriage was threatened with disruption. Roland, in particular, tried to help us through but poor Roland's own marriage was on the rocks. He was as frustrated and unhappy as myself. It seemed that a black cloud hung over our once gay, amusing circle.

I remember how during those days in Eaton Terrace, Jack Strachey used to come in and play my piano and talk to me.

One evening when he arrived he seemed very excited. He had been working until the small hours. he said, trying to find the right music for some wonderful new words that Eric Maschwitz had written. He played and sang this song to me 'These Foolish Things . . .' I was one of the first ever to hear that haunting song which eventually swept the world and is still bringing in royalties.

Apart from the winds of change that threatened my personal life, there was a general feeling of unease throughout the world. Hitler had marched into Czechoslovakia. Nobody quite knew what was going to happen next.

Then Chamberlain returned from Munich with his scrap of paper and the promise of peace which was to be so cruelly broken.

In late 1938, Arthur and I parted. Our divorce was set in motion, and I joined Neill in Egypt, but was to be there only for a short time because early in 1939, he was recalled to take his place among several other officers, skilled electrical engineers specially selected for a top-secret job. He worked on the first radar machine ever made here. It was being jealously guarded on a special site up in Felixstowe.

Arthur had given up the Eaton Terrace house. I stayed on in my London flat in Sloane Street. Arthur finally returned to Sussex where he lived until he died. He never remarried.

Eve volunteered as a V.A.D. nurse and worked as one for a year, then transferred into the A.T.S. Pat joined the W.A.A.F. Anne was still at school. They divided their leaves and holidays between their father and me.

I had no sons, yet found myself the mother of three uniformed, regimented girls on active service, living under harsh conditions in huts or military or air force quarters. They had tremendous spirit. I must say I was proud of them.

I was glad that after my life with Arthur Robins finished, we bore each other no malice. It was extremely sad in one way—but perhaps our separation was a great relief in other ways, to him as well as myself.

There was to be no world peace yet, but at least there need be no further personal conflict, and for that I was thankful. I had had more than I wanted of heartache and strain. I was anxious to begin a settled domestic life with the right man this time. It was good to find myself free to marry Neill. I found our love for each other all-absorbing.

We were married at Chelsea Register Office on the 30th October, 1939.

The Roland Pertwees held a small reception for us in their flat in Cottesmore Court, Kensington.

My girls, although sad that all was over between their parents, were very understanding. They liked Neill. Nobody could help it. He was charming, gay and friendly. They accepted him and wanted me to be happy. Their loyalty to their father never wavered and neither did I wish it to. I am firmly convinced that there should never be any question of children being asked to 'take sides' in a divorce. At no time did Arthur or I ever say one word against each other to our young family. Our differences and miseries remained our own private concern.

Neill and I had only two days' honeymoon. He had an important job and leave was not easy to get just then.

We stayed at the Dorchester and lay awake for a time listening to the distant fire of anti-aircraft guns.

London at war! My heart was heavy at the thought that my young soldier husband might soon be taken from me.

I was lucky. His first posting was not into action but to Edinburgh where he became an Instructor of Fire Control attached to the Gunners.

We left by the night train to Edinburgh, seen off by my nephew Christopher and his wife. I little guessed that it would be the last time I would ever see my beloved Christopher, but it was only a very short while after that that he was to die in the service of his country.

147

He was an R.A.F. instructor when he was killed, flying over Coventry. It was one of those terrible and needless accidents. All the barrage balloons should have been taken down when the flying instructors went up. That fatal day one balloon had been left up in error, swaying in the sunlight. Christopher's plane hit the invisible cable. He and his nineteen-year-old pupil crashed and were killed instantly.

He is buried in Coventry.

Dear Buzz. Unique, lovable rebel! I would like to quote from the last letter I received from him just before he was killed.

I had written to say that I wished he would present me with a great-niece or nephew. He replied, ironically:

'This world at war is not ready for another Brackenbury yet. I spend far too many hours in a cockpit teaching the young, but better a sore behind than a two-line mention in the Roll of Honour.'

Within a week or two, that name was, indeed, to get its 'two-line mention' in that sad, sad Roll.

Per Ardua Ad Astra.

11

THERE began for me a totally new life—so different from the old one, that sometimes it was hard for me to realise I had ever been anything but 'Mrs. O'Neill Pearson'. I soon grew used to it and to hearing myself called 'Miss Robins'—only in connection with my career.

To begin with, I went up to Edinburgh with some misgiving. I had always lived in the south and never wanted to go north—besides which, Neill and I had only just finished furnishing a delightful flat in Tite Street, Chelsea. I had hoped to live there. But I was agreeably surprised by Edinburgh. I could not but help being impressed by the beauty of the old castle standing high above the town, with the rugged hills they called 'Arthur's Seat', dark purplish green, in the background.

I used to walk up there with Nicky, my Cairn terrier, look down on the smoking chimneys and understand why they once called it 'Auld Reekie'.

I fell in love with the glorious black and white architecture of Edinburgh's Georgian Squares and Crescents, the broad streets and the monuments. I found the mighty structure of the Forth Bridge most impressive. I was fascinated by Holyrood, and there enriched my knowledge of Scottish history and particularly of Mary Stuart.

Princes Street in 1939 was gay—full of busy shops and restaurants—teeming with men on active service. Every kind of uniform could be seen. It was very cosmopolitan in those days. One heard many strange tongues spoken. The Polish Air Force was formed there. The Dutch Navy used to come into Leith Docks to refit, and their headquarters were not far from our flat, a building soon to become known as 'Dutch House'. Scottish Command held sway up in the castle where we went to some wonderful parties. Neill's Staff Headquarters were in beautiful Melville Street. He had to travel the length and breadth of Scotland in his job and I was often left alone with Nicky and an old Scottish housekeeper named Mrs. Aitken who looked after us while we were there.

I remember the first day the old Scots servant came into my service, I asked her to light the fire before breakfast, because I felt the piercing cold. I never did get used to those bitter winds which tore down Princes Street during the winter, or the lack of any real summer.

Mrs. Aitken looked at me with horror.

'A fy-er—before br-r-reakfast,' she repeated in that rather high-pitched Edinburgh voice, an accent to become so familiar to me.

'Yes,' I said.

She shook her head at me derisively.

'Ach!' she said, 'Ye're saft.'

To her I was just another Sassenach!

Soft I was, but I hardened a bit during my long sojourn in

149

Edinburgh, and I grew to love the place. Neill and I made many good friends up there.

I must say we fed well, despite the rationing—a lot better than they did in the south. And Edinburgh was a most social spot during those war years. One dined and danced on Saturday nights at de Guise in the Caledonian Hotel, and lunched in The Aperitif and attended endless cocktail parties.

There was no bombing up there except one night when a bomb that was meant for the Forth Bridge fell fatally upon the buildings of the Distillers Company! Half a million gallons of precious whisky went up in smoke. We watched the red sinister glare of the flames from our flat windows. I was told that weeping Scotsmen lay down and tried to drink the whisky as it ran in rivulets down the gutters. At four o'clock in the morning Harry Ross, Director of the D.C.I. (now Sir Henry) and a great friend of ours, rang us up and told us of his loss with considerable emotion.

The Distillers Company were unlucky. Not long afterwards half a million gallons of whisky out of bond sank in the Atlantic *en route* for America.

But these were hardly great tragedies beside the terrible catastrophic loss of human life throughout the world. Everyone tried to go on smiling and get on with the day's job. But the situation was grave and every day I seemed to hear of yet another death of one of the boys whom my girls had known and danced with just before the war.

My two brothers-in-law were now in uniform. Pat served first in India then with the Tank Corps in the Middle East. Jack, who had gone out to Nairobi, joined the King's African Rifles. Later, because he was a first-class skier, he stood to attention with that magnificent band of young skiers who were ready to defend Finland against Russia. But that particular operation never materialised.

During these years, despite the tension and the horrors all around us, I was extremely happy with my new husband. But I knew that I could not expect to go on enjoying my personal war nor had I any right to expect to do so. There had been so much happiness for me in Edinburgh, I could count myself lucky. I even had Eve stationed near me for a time, as an A.T.S. driver.

Pat, a W.A.A.F. Flight-Officer working on radar, also came up to Edinburgh on leave. The Dutch naval officers used to hold wonderful parties for the girls.

My daughters had their fair share of fun—and sorrow. Poor Pat was to lose the man who she had hoped to marry—Ken Lyons—a charming Australian Bomber Pilot who was among the thousands who never came back from 'Night Ops'.

Anne joined us in Scotland and went to a temporary school in Bridge of Allan. I wanted her to escape the constant bombing in the south. But she did not stay with us for long. Soon, she, too, left school for good and put on W.A.A.F. uniform. I felt that our old peaceful life had vanished for ever.

Neill got his Majority and we proudly exchanged the three 'pips' on his shoulder for a 'crown'. There was vague talk at H.Q. about him being sent back south to Camberley to the Staff College.

It was while we were still in Edinburgh that I came across Helen—now my greatest friend.

She was then married to an Air Force officer named Graham Mackay. Helen Mackay was a young attractive American. She worked for the W.V.S. I had gone along to her Head Office to be interviewed for a part-time job. I was at once struck by her vivid charm and personality. She was a slender woman, very smart in her green uniform, dark-haired, with beautiful sparkling eyes that narrowed to little slits when she laughed. We liked each other at first meeting and we still do. It has been a wonderful friendship that has lasted through the years. In time to come, Helen's own marriage ended. She is now married to John Tallent—stockbroker, and one of the most charming men I have ever known. 'Tally', as we call him, was an international Rugby football player, and became President of the Rugby Football Union, some twenty years after the war.

Remembering those days in Scotland brings to mind the terrible sinking by enemy action of *The City of Benares*. This liner was torpedoed on its way to Canada while carrying hun-

dreds of innocent children whose parents wished them to be
safe.

Among the passengers were my old friends the Digby Mortons, travelling to Canada on a special Board of Trade ('Britain Delivers the Goods') mission.

For nineteen hours before being finally landed by a des-
troyer at Greenock, Phyllis had sat up to her waist in icy water
in a lifeboat, holding child after child in her arms, watching all
of them die, helpless to save them.

It was an experience I could never get her to talk about, not
even when she stayed with me a few months later in Edinburgh.

One fleeting recollection from that awful night, however, I
did salvage. I quote it because it has always seemed to me a
supreme example of native Irish wit triumphing over circumstances. Like everyone else, Phyllis had fled her cabin with no
more than a snatched-up cardigan, leaving all her possessions
to go down to the bottom of the Atlantic. Among them was a
hat by Aage Thaarup, one of the then ultra-fashionable models
without any crown.

'Won't the fishes be surprised,' murmured Digby in an
effort to keep her spirits up as they sat in the water-logged
lifeboat, 'when they come across Aage's hat and find they can
swim right through it?'

12

ONE day Neill was told definitely that he was to go to
Camberley on a staff officer's course.

It was goodbye to our home in Scotland and all the friends
we had made there.

Followed a period when Neill and I lived under uncomfortable conditions in a freezing little bed-sitting-room in Camberley. I saw little of him because he had to work madly day and
night. It was rather a stiff exam. During the war, officers tried

to cram three years' work into six months.

Neill emerged triumphant at the end—but by that time we had decided that it would be a good thing for us to have a home of our own, whatever was to happen in the future.

I found one of those tiny attractive houses in Donne Place, a cul-de-sac not far from Peter Jones.

I was delighted with it and we moved in. But I lived with the fear that Neill had been 'groomed' down in the Staff College for a special job which would soon take him right away from me.

The blow fell one night in September. It was the year 1943.

Neill walked into our house and told me that he had to leave immediately. He could not tell me where he was going nor when he would be sailing. Everything was secret—hush-hush. It meant separation for us until we met again.

I was sick at heart when finally I walked with Neill down our street into Draycott Avenue. He looked so young—he was so very handsome—and he was the love of my life. He carried with him his haversack and a suitcase. It looked horribly like active service.

He kissed me goodbye. We weren't able to say much. When I returned to the house I faced a complete blank. I hadn't the slightest idea when I would see him again. We had been married for barely three years, and I'm afraid I wasn't very brave. I started to cry. I think I cried miserably for a week.

Only my little Cairn was left to console me. Everything seemed terribly lonely. The sudden wrench from the warmth of love and happiness was devastating. I had a vague notion that Neill was going overseas, and that only after the troopship sailed would he be allowed to communicate with me.

Day after day I waited, carrying on with my daily life—my work—and thinking, *tomorrow I may hear*. Suddenly, almost to my dismay, Neill telephoned from Liverpool, but not to say he could come home—only to inform me that although I had not realised it, he had been sitting all this time on that troopship, waiting to sail. They were still waiting for their convoy. It was so much time apart wasted. He could only say a few more words then it was goodbye again, and another blank wall went up. Again the heartache and uncertainty of waiting.

Not for three weeks did I hear from Neill again. Then at last I received a brief, censored postcard telling me he had reached the Gold Coast. He was to do a job as D.A.Q.M.G. in Accra.

It was another two years before he returned to me.

They seemed very long years indeed. We wrote to each other regularly but on account of the censorship there was little either of us could tell the other about our activities. We could only keep saying how much we looked forward to the end of the war and reunion.

I knew, too, that I must count myself lucky that Neill hadn't actually been sent into the area of fighting. Of the two of us I was the one in constant danger, but I refused to leave London and went on living in my little house in Chelsea all through the worst years of the bombing.

I was anxious about my girls. I rarely saw them. They were all stationed a long way away. My mother had gone down to Ross-on-Wye because her nerves would not allow her to remain with my step-father. (He was doing a war job in London.)

She was growing old. She had had a nasty operation which left her very frail. I was glad to know that she was in the country, but felt very cut off from her. My mother-in-law was also far away up in Cartmel.

Night after night when the sirens wailed their warning (how I hated the rise and fall of that sinister moaning!), I used to get into slacks and a coat, go down to my sitting-room, and sit with my little dog in my arms under my piano. I can't think of anything more ridiculous, because if a bomb had fallen, it would have got the piano *and* me! It was psychological—one just needed an obvious shelter. The Bluthner seemed more solid than anything else in my tiny house!

Those were nerve-racking days. It was unnerving for Neill, too, out in West Africa, reading about the bombing of London, and being uncertain what was happening to me. But I had no intention of being driven out of the capital by the Luftwaffe. In London I remained.

I remember another terrible night when a land-mine blew up Paternoster Row and did so much damage around St. Paul's. It completely destroyed the offices of my publisher-cousin, Walter Hutchinson. Luckily it was at night when nobody was there. It annihilated Uncle George Hutchinson's old room with its beautiful desk and famous pictures and so many souvenirs of the firm's history. There were other firms of publishers in the Row that lost millions of books that night as well.

Phyllis Digby Morton, who was a fearless type, was still going on with her daily job as editor of *Woman & Beauty*. That next morning, we walked together down Farringdon Street, our feet crunching on broken glass. We stepped over the huge hoses which the firemen were still plying. The flames of the night were not yet out.

The great dome of St. Paul's remained intact, pointing sternly to the sky. London was subdued but not vanquished. At no time did I ever sense panic in our capital. With Churchill leading us we were all confident that we were going to win the war.

13

NEVER before had I had to live so much alone. The days were full. The nights seemed long and sad. I missed my family desperately, but I could still feel amazed, and grateful to God that Neill was spared to me. There were far too many 'war-widows'. I was thankful, too, my girls stayed unharmed.

Eve was at Tilbury, firing off anti-aircraft guns, just like any man. Pat was a Flight Officer being posted from one R.A.F. station to another. Anne spent a good deal of time in the Meteorological Office down in Cornwall.

One night I had to rush to Truro Hospital when she was faced with a sudden emergency appendix operation. She recovered from this quickly, and returned to her job.

The saddest New Year's Eve I have ever spent was in 1944.

Neill was still away. I had gone down to the country to stay with a friend. We were all due to go out to a dance on December 31st, but little Nicky, my Cairn, suddenly fell ill—so ill that I had to call in a vet who diagnosed gastro-enteritis. Nicky was near to death and must not be left.

I resigned myself to the fact that I would not be going to the party. Nothing would induce me to leave my pet. My friends reluctantly left me alone. After they had gone, the house seemed very quiet. I sat on the rug in front of the fire, with Nicky lying in his basket, trying at intervals to make him swallow a little milk and brandy.

Outside it was snowing. I hardly dare move from my dog. I couldn't eat, read—or sleep. It was an all-night vigil, but in the early hours when my friends returned I could at least tell them that my dog's life was no longer in danger. He had swallowed the first spoonful and kept it down—*and* licked my hand.

Then, at last, I felt able to say '*Happy New Year!*'

In 1944, the young naval officer whom Eve was eventually to marry arrived on the scene to play an important part in her life. Charles Murray Sutton, better known to everyone as 'John', was then a Paymaster-Lieutenant-Commander in the R.N.V.R. He was exceptionally tall—6 foot, 6½ inches, with extremely fair hair and handsome blue eyes. By profession he was a chartered accountant. His parents lived at Enfield.

Neill and I had already made John's acquaintance in Cairo. He had been doing a job for the Anglo-Persian Oil Company out there. Neill had, in fact, sold John the old Bentley car which was once his most treasured possession.

We ran across John again in Edinburgh when his ship came into Leith to be refitted.

One morning I travelled with John down to London in the Edinburgh–King's Cross Express and talked, as I often did, with enthusiasm about 'my beautiful eldest daughter, Eve'. John, a confirmed bachelor, twinkled at me.

'Denise,' he said, 'don't try and marry me off to your daughter.'

He met her when she was on leave from the A.T.S. at Donne Place. They fell in love at first sight. Six months later when he returned from the job in Massawa, they made plans for their marriage.

Bombs were falling thick and fast upon London. The wedding, which we had wanted in town was re-arranged and finally celebrated in Liverpool. John was now in a shore job serving under the famous Admiral Sir Max Horton (the great man of the Western Approaches who finally put an end to the ghastly Atlantic sinkings). Max, incidentally, became one of Neill's and my dearest friends. After the war, Neill and I spent several happy holidays with Max but at the time of Eve's wedding the great Admiral was only a name to us.

Everything had to be done in a hurry in those war days. Eve got 'leave to be married'. They wouldn't release her altogether. Hastily we bought a small trousseau. Neill was still in West Africa. I was staying up in Cartmel with my mother-in-law.

The Suttons and Robins family foregathered in Liverpool. It was August, 1944. We spent the wedding eve at the Adelphi. Arthur gave his eldest daughter away. We met on friendly terms and 'received' together at the Adelphi after the wedding which took place in a little church in the Docks.

I remember feeling very sentimental, weeping, as many mothers do, during a beloved daughter's marriage ceremony. Eve looked so small all of a sudden beside her tremendously tall husband in his naval uniform.

She had decided because of the war not to be a white bride. She wore a charming bluish tweed suit that Digby Morton had made for her, and a tiny hat and veil.

The small dock-side church was filled. After the wedding, a taxi bearing bride and bridegroom was drawn with ropes, by eight naval ratings, through the streets all the way back to the Adelphi Hotel.

It was a stirring sight and a memorable day. The couple went off to Worcestershire for their honeymoon. The rest of us celebrated in the hotel, then returned to our respective homes.

After this I left Cartmel and returned to my little home in

London. Then suddenly, gloriously, V.E. Day dawned. No need for me to relate one word about it—so much has been written already by so many.

My great moment came in May, 1945 when I was awakened suddenly by a telephone call, and a voice that said, *'Hold the line, Liverpool wants you.'* My heart almost stopped beating. That could only mean one thing. *Neill had come back.* I had known that he was due to sail from West Africa in the near future, but he'd not expected it to be as soon as this.

Sure enough I heard his voice. Feeling quite stupid with joy I answered, and asked him how he was. He answered in a thick voice:

'I'm afraid I've got a ghastly cold.'

I didn't know whether to laugh or cry.

So my cold-ridden hero returned—looking a little older, a little thinner and slightly yellow from all the anti-malaria mepacrine tablets he had to take while he was on the Gold Coast.

We spent a short rapturous leave. Life seemed really to begin again for both of us.

The war with Germany was over. We had only Japan left to contend with. There were no more bombs on England. Millions of other women beside myself had got their men back and were feeling the better for it.

Shortly after this, Neill was posted to Sherborne.

The officers were stationed in Sherborne Castle which was a glorious place, and the C.O., Brigadier Kits Davis, was a friendly amusing man. It was a happy Mess in wonderful historic surroundings. I enjoyed those dinners in the Castle. I also formed an attachment, which was to last, with Maurice and Barbara Hopkinson. Maurice was then Manager of the Sherborne branch of the Midland Bank, and became my Manager when he transferred to London.

I remember many happy times down there—also a sudden sorrow when my little Cairn, Nicky, died. After six years of devotion—all through the war—I had to have him put down because of an incurable complaint. Only those who love dogs very much will know what a bitter day that was for me. He was given a fine funeral, and lies in a grave in Sherborne Castle where the Castle dogs have been buried for generations.

Neill's batman made a small wooden cross, bearing just his name 'Nicky', and for all I know it is still there. Nicky anyhow has a permanent place in my heart. It's amazing how one's pet can become an integral part of one's life. It seems to me so tragic that our dogs can remain with us for such a brief time.

I did not buy another dog for a long time.

Pat, too, had a pet with her all through the war—a charming Corgi that she called 'Heinkel'. All the dogs in the camp were named after aircraft. Heinkel comforted Pat during those dark war days. He went with her everywhere, and became quite a well-known character. He was to live until he was twelve when his loyal heart failed at last.

On 4th January, 1946, Eve came to stay with me at Donne Place. She was nearing the birth of her first child.

She woke me in the middle of the night to tell me that the pains had started. I dressed, and drove her across London in my car to the Lindo Wing, St. Mary's Hospital.

I could hardly believe that my Eve was about to become a mother. The years seemed to have gone too quickly. I was naturally anxious about her, although, in fact, she had an easy time. On the morning of January 7th she gave birth to her first daughter—Rosalind Eve.

We were all delighted. When I looked into the blue eyes of my first grandchild, I remembered the thrill of seeing her mother just after she was born. I felt amazed. This was the third generation of our family.

I was quite sorry when Eve and John and their baby returned to their own home and I had to say goodbye to them.

I wondered how long I was to be allowed to stay in Donne Place. Soon Neill, for the second time in his life, was posted to Egypt, this time to G.H.Q. as a Staff-Officer.

I had no great wish to return to the Middle East. I did not like it, but where Neill was I wanted to be. Before joining him, I nearly lost my life by having a perforated appendix followed by peritonitis.

Neill was in the Midlands on that day in March, 1946 when it all blew up. He came rushing back. At one moment I seemed well. Within two hours I was desperately ill, almost unconscious. My life was saved by a nephew of Neill's—Peter Murley (son of his half-sister Annie—daughter of old Mr. Pearson's first marriage).

Peter knew something about medicine. My secretary tried madly to get hold of a doctor but they all seemed to be on their rounds. I could think of nobody to send for but Peter. He lived nearby. When he saw me, he recognised the gravity of my condition, phoned through to a famous surgeon friend at Princess Beatrice Hospital and hung on until he got him on the line. An hour later I was in the London Clinic *and* on the operating table. It was just as well; another hour and I wouldn't be writing these memoirs. The rapidity with which such things can blow up is quite frightening. I owe my life to Peter *and* the surgeon, Kenneth Heritage.

On 23rd March, 1946, while I was in the Clinic, my brother-in-law, Pat, married an attractive girl named Sarah, eldest daughter of Sir Thomas Tomlinson. Like the Pearsons, she came from the Lake District.

The bride and bridegroom came to see me in the Clinic after the ceremony, and Sarah left her wedding bouquet on my bed.

Jack Pearson also found a wife round about this time while out in Austria—Maria, an attractive Viennese. So now all three Pearson brothers were married and their widowed mother, whom the boys in their schooldays had christened 'Blossom', left the Lake District and joined her large family in the south.

'Blossom' was quite a character. A tall, pale, plump lady—she bore little resemblance to her name, although I have every evidence from her early photographs that she was once a beautiful girl. She had a sense of humour which appealed to me, and was warm-hearted and generous to her sons. After her initial disapproval of Neill's marriage she became a firm friend of mine, and one of my most ardent 'readers'. I was very attached to 'Blossom'. I suppose I can offer no finer epitaph to a mother-in-law than to say that I still miss her.

The day came, later, when Pat fell in love with Donald Campbell-Clark, a young Scottish Squadron-Leader. He had a first-class brain and sterling character, but neither of them felt very sure that they would 'get on'.

In order to find out just how she really felt about things, Pat decided to go out to Egypt with me when I joined Neill who had already left England. He was in Cairo and delighted to have Pat with me. We set forth on what was to prove to be one of the most momentous journeys of both our lives.

Francis Gerard, the novelist, has best described what happened in one of his thrillers which he wrote later. He called it *Flight into Fear*. Certainly, it was a frightening experience for us all!

We left Poole Harbour in *The Golden Hind*, a big flying-boat which was the pride of the airline. The Captain, Dudley Trevor, was in particularly good spirits because it was his hundredth flight. He was to broadcast the fact when he reached Cairo.

14

IT was Christmas Eve.

Neill was waiting for us at a hotel in Cairo. We were to have a tremendous reunion and Christmas party. We were due to arrive in the late afternoon.

Pat and I were delighted to find Francis Gerard, his wife and infant son on board. We were a gay party. Some of the passengers were flying on to South Africa, including the Gerards who had decided to leave England for ever and were going to make a permanent home in Johannesburg.

It was a disastrous flight.

We should have come down to refuel at the island of Augusta, off the coast of Sicily. We were scheduled to get there about three p.m. Instead, we hit one bad electrical storm after another, and when darkness fell, Captain Trevor was still circling around trying hopelessly to avoid the dangerous storms and land the big flying boat before our fuel gave out. I don't think any of us really realised our danger until the steward came and told us to put on our life-jackets. Then we really did face the fact that we might all find ourselves 'in the drink'.

Mrs. Gerard was terribly air-sick; so were the others. I was lucky. I was quite well. I had to take the infant from Mrs. Gerard who in the end was quite unable to hold him a moment longer.

One often wonders what one's last thoughts would be if one knew one were about to die. Pat said that she felt too sick to care what happened. I felt surprisingly unmoved. I happened to be wearing a new mink coat. The baby was sick on it. I was really far more concerned about my mink than with the idea of dying!

Francis Gerard sat with coat off and shirt sleeves rolled up, busily writing his impressions on a portable typewriter. Once he turned to me with a grim smile.

'I want my dinner—don't you?' he asked.

It was then ten p.m. We were about six hours overdue. We had no food on board. But only Francis was hungry!

We were then over Augusta but could not land. It was pitch black. There were no guiding lights. A ninety-mile an hour gale was blowing. Rain hissed against the windows and we could see the lightning, although unable to hear the thunder. Afterwards, we learned that the B.O.A.C. staff were desperately anxious about us down below there, very uncertain as to what our ultimate fate would be.

The Captain made a forced landing with miraculous skill in that small stormy basin. We hit the sea with a crash that shivered the air-liner and sent the water shooting up over the windows. We could hear the sinister sound of lapping water behind us where the luggage was stored. We had broken one float and stay. We feared now that the liner would turn turtle and we should all drown.

Captain Trevor was magnificent. By revving up the engines, he pulled us out of the water while some of the crew sat on the one good wing in order to maintain a correct balance. After an hour a B.O.A.C. launch got across from the mainland with a crew who managed to help the passengers out through the escape hatch. Our luggage was left behind.

I don't think I realised the force of the gale until I was actually outside. It took a man on either side to hold us passengers up as we climbed into the launch.

Pat and I, and the Gerards, soaked to the skin, faced each other in the lounge of the B.O.A.C. hotel, and felt truly thankful to be alive. We had never any of us been nearer to death. We were given brandy and coffee by an apologetic staff and told that we would have to spend the night on the island but that a relief plane would take us on to Cairo in the morning.

Pat and I stared at each other blankly. It was Christmas Eve! Neill was waiting for us in Cairo; it was terribly disappointing. When we learned that all telephonic communications with the mainland had been severed by the storm and that we couldn't even get in touch with Neill, our hearts sank. He, too, would be frantically worried.

There was one woman passenger among us with a small son. He was crying bitterly. We heard him say: 'But Father Christmas thought I would be in Cairo! Now he won't know where I am!'

Later on, the storm completely subsided and the stars came out. Most of us went out. The gaily lit shops of Augusta were still open and the friendly Sicilians anxious to serve us. We all got together, bought presents and filled a stocking for the anxious little boy so he need not feel he had been forgotten by Father Christmas.

We also attended midnight Mass in Augusta Cathedral. It is a massive building. A thousand or more Sicilians were gathered there, each bearing a lighted candle. It looked beautiful and inspiring, and the singing was glorious.

One thing Pat and I remember most vividly about that night, however, was the cold. We were not prepared for it. We had expected to find ourselves in 'sunny Egypt'. Instead we were housed in what had once been a Luftwaffe Barracks in Sicily in mid-winter. It was shabby and draughty but all that

163

the B.O.A.C. could offer. We couldn't even get enough water to fill hot bottles. Our beds were hard and cold. Solemnly, Pat and I hung up our stockings and when morning broke, complained bitterly to each other that Father Christmas had obviously not been told where *we* were!

But oh, how lovely the morning looked! The sudden transition that can only take place in the Mediterranean, from cold to warmth, from storm to peace, had transformed our world. We woke to a brilliant blue sky and warm golden sunshine pouring on to our balcony where we breakfasted. Later we walked across to the waterside. The turbulent sea of last night had become a calm blue lake. The poor old *Golden Hind* lay crippled, beached on the far shore; it was a sorry sight.

Captain Trevor remained in bed suffering from shock. He was a disappointed and distressed man, so we heard. We all sent him a message of good-will and gratitude. We felt indebted to him for his magnificent mastery of the flying boat. We owed him our lives.

Soon after breakfast the relief plane came and flew us on to Cairo. It was an uneventful trip in perfect weather. At last we landed on the Nile. Neill met us at Cairo airport, overjoyed to see us. He had spent a bad night, he said. He went down to meet the *Golden Hind* at the appointed time only to be told that there had been a catastrophe beyond which he learned nothing more for many hours.

It was Pat's first glimpse of Cairo, although by this time I knew it well. She had to learn, as I had done, that it could be unpleasantly cold during the winter.

We stayed in a huge hotel with tessellated floors and rooms leading out of each other through tall open archways. Everything was draughty. A *khamsin* was blowing, driving clouds of dust along the streets. We spent an uncomfortable night.

At this time, the situation in Cairo was tricky. The unpopular King Farouk was already sowing the seeds of revolt (although then he didn't yet know it). There was seething discontent throughout the Egyptian army and a hostile feeling against British troops stationed in Cairo. Neill and Pat and I were there only a few weeks before we were ordered down to the Canal Zone where the British had hastily erected Army quarters in Fayid, on the shores of the Great Bitter Lake.

I did not like the idea of occupying one of the restricted officers' quarters in that vast camp. It would have been hopeless for my literary work, so we found and rented a villa in Ismailia on the banks of the Suez Canal. Flanked on the other side by the Sweet Water Canal, it was a beautiful little town, full of flowering trees; but the climate was bad. The heat in midsummer became insupportable to me. The humidity was so high.

Pat, after a few weeks, bade us goodbye and flew back to England, confident then that Donald was the only man in the world for her.

Not long after her return, they were married up in Glasgow —a wedding which I unfortunately had to miss because Pat wanted it to be a quiet one, and thought it would be silly for me to travel all that way back just when I had settled down in Ismailia.

Looking back, I don't think I ever really 'settled'. Army life in the Middle East (or anywhere else) did not suit my temperament. I don't drink, smoke or play games. I was a bit 'out of it' among the Army wives who enjoyed that sort of life. The old urge for my literary work was upon me. I missed London life.

I had no time for 'elevenses' with the others who gathered either in the Club or on what they called 'The French Beach', where everybody bathed. Most of them enjoyed it and so did the hundreds of children who seemed to thrive despite the difficult climate.

I liked the French Club, run mainly for the canal pilots under the direction of a big handsome, affable Greek, named George Papadakis.

I put him into my novel *Khamsin*. He is now married to an American girl and lives in New York. He always signs his letters to me 'George of Khamsin' which has a slightly 'Kitchener of Khartoum' flavour! We had many amusing dinner parties and dances in that club, always at a special table reserved for us by 'George of Khamsin'.

I think I might have quite enjoyed my life in Egypt had it not been for the fact that my health began to crack up. I suffered from a nasty complaint which they call *Trigeminal Neuralgia*. An excruciating pain runs from the top of the skull across one eye and down the cheek and neck. It spoiled my fun in Egypt, and lasted for about two years. Mercifully it vanished as suddenly as it had come, just as one specialist had told me it might do. While I was having acute attacks I was good for nothing. I went home every summer to stay with one or other of my girls.

I hated these partings from my husband but felt he would be better without me during the torrid summers when I was so much worse.

15

IN 1948 I went home especially to stay with Eve and John who were then living in a tiny house in Enfield. Eve was awaiting the birth of her son, Murray. He was born on the 3rd July. Soon afterwards, the Sutton family moved to Brookmans Park where they stayed for some time. (They have now a charming old Sussex house in Cowfold—a village not far from Slaugham.)

It was eight years later that his little sister Annabel was born. She is now a tall girl with blue eyes and long fair hair. At the age of seventeen she is quite an accomplished pianist and guitarist and can also play the organ. At this moment of writing she is just completing a session at the Connaught Theatre, Worthing where she has been a trainee student and does mysterious and useful jobs on the stage when the curtain is down. It appears that like her sister Rosalind she has a flair for teaching and that will be her career.

In less than a year after Pat's marriage, my youngest daughter, Anne, also decided to plunge into matrimony.

We all had expected her to take up a musical career. She was a good pianist and had qualified at the Trinity College in

London for both piano and clarinet. Like her grandfather before her, she sang in the Bach Choir. Suddenly at a party, she met Romance with a capital 'R' (like something out of one of her mother's own stories, she said) and it was to be marriage instead of a career.

Peter Chadwick who caused this upheaval in her life was a slim good-looking boy. A commercial artist. He seemed to possess all the qualities she had ever wanted in a man and she didn't mind the fact that he had no money.

They married very much on love and hope. I, slightly stunned, received a cable while I was still out in Egypt telling me that they were married.

I was sad to miss the weddings of my two youngest daughters but that was a price I had to pay for my remarriage. I had a duty to Neill as well as to my girls and I could not keep on leaving him. Indeed, I did not want to.

I have found that being a grandmother brings a particular warmth and joy into life. I was glad when Neill was posted back to England so we could finally see more of the young family.

In 1949 we returned to our little house in Chelsea, but shortly afterwards left it—this time for good. Neill was destined to remain in the Army for only one more year.

Now my daughter, Pat, also busily turning out romantic novels, and Don, her husband, bought a house a few miles from us. This was a great joy to me—still more so when they decided to adopt a little boy.

Ever since she had been married, Pat had been hoping for a child, but none had come. She adored children and not having had one was a bitter disappointment to her.

One day, together, we went up to the National Adoption Home. After long months of waiting, Pat and Don had succeeded in finding the little baby they had wanted for such a long time. A son. In this way, the delightful boy who was christened Iain, entered our family.

Two years later Pat and Donald adopted a little daughter, Nicola (also called Denise, after me). The adoptions have been a tremendous success. When Pat unexpectedly brought a son of her own (whom they called Graeme) into the world, Iain and Nicola still held firm places in all hearts.

Nicola is now a beautiful twenty-two year old working in a boutique, and her brother Iain works for Schroders, the merchant bankers.

Anne's family has increased to seven. The eldest boy and girl, David and Belinda, are married. Belinda has a little girl, so I have become a great-grandmother.

We were living in Buckinghamshire in those days, and I was working so hard that I needed a first-class secretary to keep up with my dictation speed. It was then that Phyllis Gartside came into my life. Not only is she an efficient secretary but a charming personality. She is still with me—after twenty-three years—very much a family friend now. 'Phyl', as we call her, when she first started to work for me cleverly divided her time between my exacting career and her two children, Jill and Peter, who were at boarding school. (Like my own girls, they are now grown up. Jill is married and living in Australia with three children. Peter is now a successful business executive with a daughter of his own. She bears the enchanting name of Leontine.)

I have no hesitation in saying I don't know what I should do without Phyl!

But back now to the early days when she came to work for me.

Finally I found my ideal London home—a small Regency house in Caroline Terrace, which leads out of Eaton Terrace. Painted white, with green shutters and window-boxes full of pink ivy leaf geraniums tumbling over themselves, it was enchanting. We settled down there.

In 1952, Hutchinsons published my 100th novel. We celebrated this with a big party in London. I felt, I suppose, rather like a cricketer who has made his century. My husband gave me one hundred pink roses. It was a thrill to receive so many of my literary friends and associates, but impossible for me to name all the guests. I do remember, however, being photographed with my old friend Donald Gray whom I first met in Egypt when he was filming in *The Four Feathers*. Greta Gynt was with us. Louis Golding arrived and Charles Creed, and Nancy Spain, who in the *Daily Express* described the room as *'looking like a vast wedding cake'* with me, *'swathed in rich navy blue satin from Digby Morton, looking like a bride'*.

The great surprise of the evening was a miraculous cake which my three daughters had had specially made in the shape of the 100th book, *Strange Meeting*. The title and author's name were raised in sugar. I cut the cake with the help of my daughter, Patricia, and my old mother (then in her eighties) who had travelled from Brighton especially for the event. It was positively her first and last appearance at any of my parties. Godfrey Winn was also present with *his* mother. It was to be her last appearance, too, although Godfrey and I little dreamed it. Godfrey proposed my health and made a wonderful speech in praise of my long years of hard work, and I felt grateful to him and to all the good friends I have made during my career.

Later, Christina Foyle helped me celebrate the event at her 242nd Literary Luncheon. They called it 'Love Will Find A Way'. I was the main speaker. Many well-known 'romantic novelists' were present—Ursula Bloom, Barbara Cartland, Ruby M. Ayres, Berta Ruck and dozens of others. Godfrey Winn was Chairman and once again made an excellent speech. *'Don't ever be cynical,'* he said, *'and dismiss the work that romantic novelists do as unimportant.'*

I lived a full and interesting literary life in London. Suddenly, one of the most valued and interesting of my friends, Joan Werner Laurie, came into my life. She was at the time living in a mews cottage with that energetic and scintillating character, Nancy Spain. They held a Guy Fawkes party, to which we were invited.

Not long after that party I heard the first murmur about the launching of a new woman's magazine which Miss Laurie—better known to her friends as Jonnie—had for some time been planning.

To those who do not know her well, Jonnie may look slight and delicate, but the steady observant blue eyes show that amazing strength and driving force that lie behind the apparent fragility. When *She* came on to the market for the first time, it proved something of a revolution in magazines for women.

It was *different*! It was an instant success and has continued to be one, with an ever-rising circulation.

I shall never forget the exciting evening when I first went to Clareville Grove to see Jonnie, and she showed me the original 'dummy' of this literary 'infant-prodigy'. I was offered the job of answering the Problem Page letters. I gave this page the title: 'Straight From The Shoulder'. It was a great joy to me and over the years has proved a stimulating job. Letters come from all over the world. They bring me in close contact with human beings in all kinds of trouble. It is my privilege to help and counsel.

Among the sad and sometimes tragic letters, there are of course the amusing ones. One which I can never remember without a smile, went like this:

'Dear Denise,

I am the mother of four children. Now I am going to have a fifth child to a bus conductor I fell for. Please what am I to do because he's changed his route! ...'

Not an easy one to answer. I answered it privately—not on my page!

I have known Joan Werner Laurie as a personal friend as well as an editor for quite a while now. In both capacities I find her delightful. Neill and I have shared several stimulating holidays abroad with her and the racing motorist, Sheila Van Damm, who is another remarkable woman.

It was a great sorrow to me that I had to add a tragic paragraph to this part of my story. Jonnie Werner Laurie and Nancy Spain were killed in that grim air crash over the Grand National Race Course at Aintree on 21st March, 1964. I felt I had lost two dear friends, and where Jonnie is concerned, one of my nearest and dearest. The world has been a sadder place for me and for many others without these friends who used to share a home, and who died together.

170

In 1957 I had re-joined the publishing house of Hodder and Stoughton, who had, in fact, published my first two novels in the long, long ago. The first on the new list was the novel I think I like best out of my many—*The Noble One*. We had a wonderful party at the Savoy to launch it. I found extra pleasure in writing this book because it is not one of my usual romances but the story of a stag—and the love of the girl and the game-warden who saved him from death. The scene is laid in the forests up above Lake Coniston. I went there in person to stay with the game-warden and his wife, and learned what I could about these fine, brave animals that roam the hills.

I have always felt acute antipathy towards stag-hunting. My novel was to be something of a protest against the brutality shown not only by so-called sportsmen who are inadequate shots, but by poachers who have no right to shoot at all, and often leave the maimed deer to suffer a slow, agonising death.

In 1954, soon after her eighty-second birthday, my mother died.

I was with her in her flat in Hove until the end. While I sat beside her, watching that greatest of all scourges destroy her vigour and looks, I felt bitterly resentful. I knew that she had reached a great age and could ask little more of Time; but it seemed so sad that she was so well in every other way—so mentally alert for her age—yet must die. Neither deafness, blindness nor any of the miseries of senility had touched her.

All our past differences when we were both younger seemed to vanish completely during those last days. Her death brought me real sorrow.

After she died she looked startlingly like the mother I remembered while in her forties. There was not a line on her face. That smile that had charmed so many during her lifetime, still curved her lips. She was amazingly young and beautiful.

After I left her, I found myself wondering where she had gone; wondering about death, after-life, and what lies in store for us all.

Mother had many devoted friends. Letters poured in, full of sympathy and regret. At her own wish she was cremated. My step-father was now alone. I knew that mother would be sadly missed by everybody for she was a great character and courageous right to the end. I feel thankful that we 'buried the hatchet' and that for ten years before her end I did as much as I could for her.

In 1958 just before Neill and I left Caroline Terrace to make a final return to Sussex, my daughters told me that their father, also had been taken gravely ill. He was in the Middlesex Hospital having a major operation.

His life was coming to an end.

He expressed a wish to see me. I went along to the hospital with Eve. Poor Arthur had been struck down by that same cruel malady that had taken my mother—still only in his early sixties; too young to die.

I spent several days sitting beside him. It was as though the years between us rolled back. We were friends again, and I like to think that my presence brought him some comfort.

He died just before Christmas Day—bravely—still joking. I know it was a great grief to my three girls and to many of his friends on the Baltic.

Neill also suffered a personal loss that year. Old Blossom, his mother, died peacefully, but suddenly, at the age of seventy-seven. Her end was a shock to Neill and his brothers. No matter how old our mothers grow, it must always be a shock, this severance from the strongest and most important blood-tie of them all.

It was not long after old Blossom's death that Neill and I began to feel the task of living in London too much for both of us. We seemed to have been caught up in the slip-stream of the terrific pace at which one can live in the great capital. Neill, brought up in the Lake District, craved for more fresh air. We both felt an urge to return to the country.

Neill was suddenly given the opportunity to work in partnership with a friend in a wrought-iron industry in Brighton. This interested him. We felt that it would suit us both to live in Sussex.

It was in 1958 that I was given the chance to buy back my beautiful home, Furnace Pond Cottage, in Slaugham. Neill fell in love with it, too. It was a temptation we couldn't resist. For me it seemed wonderful. I had done so much to the place twenty years ago and made it so perfect for my children. So much of my hard-earned money had gone into it—so much time and thought. It would be a terrific thrill to return.

So Neill and I moved in. The *Daily Express* printed a large photograph of the house and swimming-pool right across the centre page, with the headline '*Denise Robins Returns To The House Of Her Dreams*'.

Harold Keeble, who was then on the *Express*, told me that this photograph was so strikingly beautiful that the printers hung it on the wall in their own room, and for all I know, it is still there!

1959 gave us that marvellous hot summer when we had the sunshine from April until the end of October. It was a splendid welcome back to Furnace Pond.

I had the continual joy of watching my grandchildren dive into the pool which had been made for their mothers. The garden was glorious. I began to take an active interest in roses, and ever since have made them my hobby.

Two years later I was to lose yet another great pet.

Dingo, my beloved Australian, had to be put to sleep because of a painful kidney disease. He was a game little dog, but unfortunately, being a fighter he got into serious trouble. One of his many battles was with a Boxer six times his size! The dire result was that Dingo retired with seven fearful wounds. He nearly died. He was pulled through by that wonderful veterinary surgeon (now retired) Mr. Lloyd-Jones. 'Buster' Lloyd-Jones was a genius with dogs. People came to him from all over the world. He is sadly missed in the profession, although we still see him as a friend. He saved Dingo on several other occasions.

Then another pet—Gaston, a miniature Belgian Griffon.

Gaston wound himself completely round my heart. His coat had the colour and sheen of a light chestnut. He had endearing ways and huge melting dark eyes. He could prance round the floor on his hind legs as though he were circus-trained. At the same time, my daughter Pat bought another Griffon, Gigi, Gaston's female cousin. When they met they ran round together and, as a team, looked adorable.

Gaston distinguished himself by getting lost on Ashdown Forest one summer. He was missing for a whole week. I have seldom been more miserable and apprehensive. I made count-less enquiries. I offered a reward of £50. I alerted every pos-sible service including the A.A., the R.A.C., the R.S.P.C.A., the police and every local kennels or vet. The London and southern newspapers helped. Gaston suddenly became famous.

I couldn't sleep at night, missing that little warm creature who used to curl into a small ball on my bed. I was terrified that he might have fallen into the wrong hands or, alterna-tively, been run over and killed.

At the end of an anguished week, after receiving all kinds of telephone calls about 'strays' that had been found but which were never Gaston, I chartered a helicopter from Gatwick Air-port to hunt for the dog. The Captain said he could fly fairly low over the scrub and sight a small moving creature. If he thought one looked like a Griffon, he would signal us. 'Us' meant a dozen or more friends and relations stationed around the forest roads waiting to move in if and when Gaston was found.

Pat, of course, joined in the search. She was then living nearby in Ashurst Wood, and had gone out with Gigi, calling and calling, hoping that Gaston would hear her voice or pick up Gigi's scent.

It was an exciting affair but I ended the day in tears. No Gaston. The passenger on the helicopter, Phyl's son, Peter Gartside, had seen nothing. I began to fear that I would never recover my lost pet.

On the Saturday of that wretched week, I happened to be holding a party for my granddaughter Rosalind—then just six-teen. I did not wish to disappoint her, so the party took place, but I felt wretched while I dressed. I could hardly bear to glance at Gaston's water-bowl and rug.

It was seven-thirty. The party had just commenced—all the nice young things had come and told me how sorry they were about Gaston. Then the telephone bell rang. I picked up the receiver without enthusiasm. It had rung so often that week, and never with good news. A man's voice asked me my number then asked: 'Have you by any chance lost a little red pug?'

My heart almost stopped beating. I said: 'Do you mean a *Belgian griffon?*'

He said that he didn't really know what the breed was, but he had found a little emaciated creature on a heap of mowings at the bottom of his garden, and it looked like a pug.

'He has a yellow collar on and a disc bearing your telephone number,' he said.

So Gaston had been found—at last!

One day, during the summer of 1963, my dear friend, Roland Pertwee, died. He had become an old man suffering from that painful and harassing complaint, bronchial asthma, which had long since taken him away from the London life he used to love. He had settled down in Kent with Kitty, his young devoted wife.

For so many wonderful years he had been not only my close friend but my literary counsellor. I never somehow imagined life without him.

He was still a vigorous man until the end, and went on writing, and painting, which was his hobby. I spoke to him on the telephone when he was so gravely ill. He said:

'I feel as though I'm going down a dark difficult road, but I've got to find my way out of it, haven't I, Denisey?'

'Yes, and you will,' I said.

Roland had always found the way out of his difficulties. He was so resourceful. But this last effort was too much for him. His tired heart couldn't stand up to the strain it had had to take during the last few years.

I miss him sorely. I always will.

I have lost many more loved ones in recent years.

In 1961 it was an unexpected blow when my beloved god-son, Adrian Griffith, died at the age of thirty-four. The youngest son of my close friend Dr. Maud Griffith, he was all set for a splendid career; he became one of the youngest F.R.C.S.s on record and was in Chicago finding out about American hospital life when the mortal blow was struck at him. He flew home to Barts for a major operation.

Of all the romances I have ever written about none could be more poignant and beautiful than the love-story of Adrian and Catherine. Adrian had left Barts and made a temporary recovery. He fell in love with Catherine Wilson who was singing at Glyndebourne. She is very beautiful, and not only has she long red hair and a flawless face, but an exceptional voice. She had started to sing in opera in 1957 and when Adrian first met her, she was already established.

It was a case of love at first sight between these two brilliant, idealistic people. Catherine knew that Adrian had only a year, or even less to live, but she married him and she looked after him until he died. His courage was phenomenal—so was hers.

I remember when I visited him at Barts one day soon after his operation, he said to me:

'I do not mind dying, Denise; what I hate is the waste of all that I have learned. I was just beginning to prove myself as an E.N.T. specialist and I had hoped to help suffering humanity.'

Yes, it was a tragic waste, and unending sorrow to those who loved him. Catherine wished him to live those last months of his life in the *milieu* he had chosen; the little home he had ardently desired. He had bought a small attractive house for her in Islington. It was especially perfect for Catherine when she was working at Sadler's Wells, and for him not too far from Barts.

The last time I visited them there I could see that my godson had not much longer to live. But still he laughed and joked and showed an indomitable spirit. He was so proud of the antiques and pictures he had collected, so pleased with all the wedding presents. He made plans for the future, deliberately turning his back on the death which relentlessly threatened him.

He asked Catherine to play and sing for me. She did so—

with a brave gaiety, which hid her sorrow. When I said good-bye to Adrian I was heavy hearted—sure that it was for the last time. I felt not only the pain of Catherine's heart-break but the cruelty of a Fate which could take so young and fine and useful a life so quickly.

I don't know who had the greatest courage—the one who died or the wife who watched and smiled and went on singing for him—filling the house with music, with gaiety, with friends; the fine mother who adored him and took the bitter blow of his loss with such admirable fortitude.

It is true to say of Adrian Griffith:

'*Whom the gods love die young.*'

16

A FEW years ago, Neill joined a firm of stockbrokers, a business which suits him admirably and in which he is greatly interested. He has also become a great backgammon enthusiast. He enjoys both that and bridge enormously.

I seem to enjoy doing all sorts of different things. T.V., broadcasting, appearing on panels, speaking here, there and everywhere, going to literary luncheons—and the rest. I find these things stimulating, but most of all I enjoy my gardening and the roses which are my speciality.

Over long years I have talked on *Woman's Hour*. Most of these talks have been produced by Anthony Derville—always most charming and helpful. I have met many interesting personalities on that programme—such as Janet Quigley and Joanne Scott-Moncrieffe. I never feel nervous of the microphone. I like being able to talk to the tens of thousands who are good enough to want to hear me. I have made many friends and received many letters from them.

I also like T.V. and find it a good medium for expressing one's thoughts and feelings. I have always enjoyed sparring in front of the cameras with my various 'inquisitors'.

I particularly enjoyed playing in the game *Dotto* which was such a success a few years ago. I went up to Birmingham to appear on this programme and was lucky enough to get through three nights of answering questions on General Knowledge, and guessing the names of the great men whose faces were outlined in dots on the screen. It won me fifty pounds. It was a lot of fun.

I've enjoyed all the personalities whom I've met and worked with on T.V.; particularly men like Cliff Michelmore and Eamonn Andrews. My daughter, Patricia, and I once appeared together on a panel in the Midlands and I've been 'shot' several times with my friend, Barbara Cartland. Nevertheless it is a horribly revealing process and unless the lighting is right it can make you look pretty grim. I remember my very first show which I wrote for a woman's programme and which ran for several weeks. It was called *How They Said It*, and was all about famous proposals of marriage. After the first show I went back home and asked my old housekeeper—Harriet Lemon (a delightful character who was with us for ten years) how I appeared to her. Her answer was frank:

'Madame, it didn't flatter you. You looked *horrible*!'

All the same I find the hectic feverish atmosphere of the studios stimulating, and hope for the best as far as my face is concerned!

Sometimes it is difficult for me to remember that I have been at this writing game for forty years, and still have the desire to write.

I remember saying in jest to my daughter Pat that when I die I wish to be cremated and my ashes strewn over my typewriter which is then to be hurled into the sea. She laughed:

'What a waste of a good typewriter, Mum!'

I've come to the conclusion that she was right!

One of my great friends—and one of the shining personalities of our day—is Christina Foyle. A slight, dark-haired, bright-eyed young woman, she most ably took over the terrific responsibility of running the great firm of W. & G. Foyle. I have had the pleasure of speaking at one of her now famous lunches at the Dorchester. For many long years I have attended these happy lunches and through them met many interesting, unforgettable people.

Not long ago Christina and her husband, Ronald Batty, went to Japan. When they came back to their English country home in Essex, Ronnie built a Japanese tea house, with every detail correct, just as he had seen and admired in Tokyo.

It stands there in his garden now, like a small piece of Japan —exquisitely made, correctly designed, with its beautiful wood, silk sliding panels, concealed lighting—all so pure and cool, and in such perfect taste. When Neill and I were taken down to see it, we had to shed our shoes on the verandah before going inside. In true Japanese fashion we sat on cushions around the lacquered table, drinking our tiny cups of tea. We looked out upon a waterfall, little bridges and a garden full of flowering shrubs that might have come straight out of a Japanese picture book. It produces an extraordinary sense of peace. One can relax there for a long time in silent contemplation, and not wish to do anything else.

Many times while old William Foyle was alive, Neill and I used to go down to Beeleigh Abbey. I never failed to be thrilled by the fabulous collection of old books and documents which Mr. Foyle bought during his lifetime. He was very fond of my husband. Along the top floor of the Abbey, he had set up an old toy steam-train. He loved to run this train with Neill. The pair of them took a schoolboy's pleasure in playing with it. One day there was a minor explosion. They came downstairs both looking slightly crestfallen.

They had blown it up!

In 1961, Alex Stuart, well known as a writer of light fiction, and I, founded the Romantic Novelists Association. I was elected President. Barbara Cartland was one of the Vice-Presidents. She is a great friend of mine. We have now both resigned, but I often meet the glittering, glamorous Barbara.

While I was President, A. P. Herbert was my Guest of Honour at our very first dinner. He spoke to us as the great champion he is of the rights of novelists who, unlike the composers of songs, receive not a penny from the libraries who handle so many millions of their books. In 1964, we had the late Ian Fleming as our Guest of Honour, the great James Bond himself! He told me that he felt a bit out of place among all the 'romantic ladies' but I assured him (as I have done so many of those who criticise) that the word 'romance' does not necessarily stand only for sentimental love but for deeds of chivalry, and for all kinds of adventure, an atmosphere which might be found even in an Ian Fleming thriller.

17

ONE reporter who interviewed me asked me if I had found the life of a writer a 'bed of roses'?

My reply was that, on the contrary, it has been strewn with thorns. I have loved every minute of my working life. I still love my work but it always requires enormous mental and physical effort. The hours of concentration can be a strain on both nerves and eyesight. I thoroughly agree with that sadly-missed journalist Nancy Spain who once wrote these words:

'Do not be led away by the staggeringly high financial reward. There is one enormous disadvantage. A novelist is lonely.'

I think I have spoken about that loneliness a great many times in this autobiography. The creative artist is invariably a lonely person. As far as the 'staggeringly high reward' is concerned, that is an exaggeration except in the case of the top bestsellers. They are heavily taxed and have many expenses connected with their careers.

For my own success I am eternally grateful to those who have helped me 'get there', and to my readers. Whether I have lain on a bed of roses or walked on a path of thorns, my work has certainly brought me the greatest satisfaction.

Life rushes by with almost frightening speed. How long will it continue for me? Who knows?

I was talking one day to Robin Beare—that fine plastic surgeon who used to work in such close co-operation with Sir

Archibald McIndoe. Robin and his wife, Iris, are great friends of mine. He often reminds me of Roland because of his brilliant conversation and extraordinary flair for imitation. We were discussing the Corneal Graft Eye Bank at the Queen Victoria Hospital where Robin works. When I learned about the demand for 'eyes' after death, I looked into the matter. I decided that if one could help to give sight to another human being in danger of going blind, it would be a wonderful thing. It took my husband some little time to agree. There is, after all, a certain amount of gloom surrounding the idea of a body being disturbed after death. But gradually Neill came to think as I do—what does it matter what happens if one can pass on such a priceless gift as sight where it is most needed? So I signed the necessary papers and afterwards wrote a verse which has been read at many of the Corneal Graft Crusades. It is with this small poem that I would like to end my chapter:

> When I shall die, 'twill be as though the light
> Of dawn will break to pierce the grieving night
> Of death. No death, indeed, for me.
> Through other eyes, made whole by mine, I'll see.
> Through other eyes reject my final pain
> And start upon the March of Time again.
> How sweet to know that as I give up breath
> This miracle will prove—there is no death.
> And one, at least, whom I shall leave behind
> Need never dread the darkness of the blind!

18

In 1964 we decided to sell our beautiful Furnace Pond Cottage and move back to Haywards Heath. My husband was now going up to the City and it was better that he should be near a station. Haywards Heath could offer a splendid service for commuters, so we returned to Haywards Heath where I used to live when my children were small. First of all to a little early Victorian house on Muster Green while we looked for a more permanent home. This we found in 1971 and here we are now living. Our house is a really splendid example of Victorian architecture with high light rooms and a lovely walled garden leading into the Recreation Grounds, so we feel we are still living in the country, and that we really do not want to move again.

Once again I have had to say goodbye to a great pet—my little Griffon Gaston died, and later on I bought a small Yorshire terrier whom we call 'Button'. Button has for quite a few years now been a great joy to us. He is a most amusing character. Long may he live!

I have been able to continue with my gardening and have planted many more rose trees, although this present garden was full of magnificent azaleas and rhododendrons when we came. A great landmark is a colossal Southern Californian Pine Tree which spreads its wonderful dark green branches right over our wall, and the pavement in front of our house. It has a Tree Preservation order, and from the look of it, the pine will outlive us all!

Another interesting feature of this garden is what they call a 'Strawberry Tree', in other words an Arbutus. I've often seen them in the South of France, but rarely over here. As I write in cold, frosty December, it is scarlet with little ripe strawberries, and, a complete paradox, little white spring flowers—a rare combination. The joy of any horticulturist, of course.

Looking back over the last three years or more, life has been good for me as a writer. My paperbacks seem to sell in tens of thousands all over the world and have reached beyond the ten million mark. Possibly I can say that my bestseller up-to-date is *House of the Seventh Cross*—a novel about Majorca, which has had its 100,000th printing. I was inspired to write this story after staying in Pollensa in my brother-in-law's house— one of the old attractive buildings high up above the ancient village. It was full of atmosphere, and the significance of the title was drawn from the fact that it is one of many houses leading up to a Monastery halfway up the side of a mountain.

The rough roadway is known as the Calvario. Every Easter, there is a religious festival in Pollensa and the pilgrims stop to pray before the Stations of the Cross, as they climb up the three hundred and sixty-five stone steps. My brother-in-law's house is marked with the *Seventh* Cross.

It is interesting to me to receive wonderful posters from the publishers who print my books in Finland. They seem to like romance in Finland, to say nothing of Africa and India where many of my friends find my paperbacks in the most unexpected native quarters. One of my great joys is the letters I receive from so many of my faraway readers.

Hodder and Stoughton, my publishers, have now founded the 'Coronet Romance Club' of which I am President. I retired from the R.N.A. a few years ago. The Coronet Club magazine has also found its way to the four corners of the earth, and through this I get a rewarding fan-mail.

In 1965, my friend Christina Foyle gave me a Luncheon at the Dorchester to celebrate the publication of my Autobiography. It was one of the great thrills of my life. Over seven hundred people were present. Robert Morley, that inimitable humorist, was Chairman and he made the most delicious speech. I sat on his right and on my left was my old colleague Beverley Nichols.

There were so many wonderful Guests of Honour I haven't space to mention them all, but among the best-known, Eamonn Andrews, Jessie Matthews, Alan Melville, Michael and Jon Pertwee, Barbara Cartland, and that wonderful driving motorist, Sheila van Damm. It was good to see them all.

I didn't find it easy to make a speech, with all these brilliant people listening to me, but somehow I got through it, and was grateful for my wonderful reception.

I always go to the Foyle Lunches. I think that they are the most stimulating and interesting gatherings of the day. Christina Foyle is a highly intelligent and imaginative woman, and Neill and I value her and her husband as friends.

We nearly always spend one weekend in the year either at her private house, or at the famous and beautiful Beeleigh Abbey where visitors can see some of the most rare and interesting First Editions that could be found in any library, in the world.

Since the last edition of my Autobiography was published, my family has increased. Now I have a little great-granddaughter, Pippa, who makes my youngest daughter, Anne, a grandmother. Her eldest girl Belinda Pauline, was married six years ago. They do grow, these children! Which leads me to speak of another very romantic marriage between my granddaughter Rosalind and a gifted artist from Czechoslovakia.

Rosalind spent three years at Bristol University where she took a Degree in Classics and Drama. After this she visited Prague because she was interested at that time in the Marionette Theatres for which Czechoslovakia is famous. There she met Milan Ivanič, a young gifted painter, and they fell in love. They were married in Sussex not long afterwards.

I never go away without finding some fresh inspiration for a new novel. The new one is about Madeira. My husband and I stayed at the famous old Reid's Hotel, and this with its glorious hanging gardens and wonderful view of the sea I have described in a novel which is entitled *Dark Corridor*. Already I am beginning to think about yet another book. As I grow older I may write more slowly but I can't ever see myself saying goodbye to my pen or my typewriter while there is still a breath of life in me!

Recently I found it great fun being in *This is Your Life* with the inimitable Eamonn. It was Pat Reid's life—Major Reid of 'Escape From Colditz'. I was present by virtue of the fact that I had known Pat and his family for so long. During this show I found the meeting between the escaped English prisoner and his one-time German Security Officer very touching. On the stage the old enemies embraced each other like comrades. The German, now in his eighties, hugged Pat and said with a twinkle, '*Ach—but tonight you will not outvit me!*'

One B.B.C. broadcast in which I featured and enjoyed, took place in the memorable year of 1973. I chose my eight records for Roy Plomley on 'Desert Island Discs', and during our session he mentioned that he had heard that I usually dictated my novels 'off the cuff'. He then invited me to do so right there between records. I must say I had a moment of panic but managed it. So the idea for *Dark Corridor* was born. I dictated the first paragraph of it to Roy and it is those very words that open my 1974 novel.

This summer, my old friend Jon Pertwee, came down to see us with his lovely family. I invited all the local girls and boys —children of my friends—all crazy to meet 'Dr. Who' in person. One little boy as soon as he saw Jon, recognised him but his lower lip trembled as he looked anxiously past him and said, '*Oh! but you haven't brought your Daleks!*'

Needless to say Dr. Who was a huge success.

So time marches on. At this very moment of writing poor old England is facing a lot of trouble and we are all wondering when we will begin to feel peaceful and progressive again. Oh well, the day must come!

I don't mind what '*they*' think. *I* know and so do we all that we are people who believe in England and whether Britannia still 'Rules the Waves' or not, she will certainly never allow any of us to become *Slaves*.

On that comforting thought, I would like to end my Autobiography.

INDEX

Agate, James, 137
Allied Press, 105
Amalgamated Press, 104
Andrews, Eamonn, 178, 183, 184
Artist's Model, The, 104
Ashworth, Joan, 115
Avenue Road, St. John's Wood, 15, 66
Ayres, Ruby M., 135, 169

Bankhead, Tallulah, 135
Batty, Ronald, 179
Beare, Iris, 181
Beare, Robin, 180–1
Beeleigh Abbey, 179, 183–4
Bell, Silvia, 20
Belmonte (toreador), 125
Bennett, Arnold, 136
Bernstein, Henri, 123
Berry, Gomer (Lord Kemsley), 16
Best, Edna, 119, 122, 123
Betty's Paper, 106
Bloom, Ursula, 136, 169
Boon, Charles, 124, 136
Bow Bells, 106
Brackenbury, Christopher, 147–8
Brighton, 73–5, 78–80, 83, 91, 92, 98, 107, 109–12, 114
Broad, Nurse, 107
Buckner, R. A., 60

Cairo, 139–42, 161, 163–5
California, 37–40
Camberley, Staff College, 151, 152
Campbell-Clark, Donald, 161, 165, 167
Campbell-Clark, Graeme, 168
Campbell-Clark, Iain, 167, 168
Campbell-Clark, Nicola, 167, 168

Campbell-Clark, Patricia, *see* Robins, Patricia
Caroline Terrace, 168, 172
Carroll, Sydney, 16, 74, 135–6
Cartland, Barbara, 169, 178, 179, 183
Chadwick, Anne, *see* Robins, Anne
Chadwick, Belinda, 168, 184
Chadwick, David, 168
Chadwick, Peter, 167
Chamberlain, Neville, 146
Chester Terrace, Regent's Park, 20, 22, 24
Christian Science, 25–9, 32, 54
Colbourne, Dorothy (Dorothy Pertwee), 111, 117, 119
Colbourne, Geoffrey, 111, 114, 117
Colbourne, Michael, 111, 119
Colon (Panama), 42
Corneal Graft Eye Bank, 181
Cornwell, George Chesterton, 16, 50, 74
Cornwell, Jemima (*née* Redpath), 16
Cornwell, Mary, 50, 74, 78
Cornwell-Clyne, Adrian (brother of D. R.), 18, 20, 25, 26, 30, 54, 61–2, 65, 80
Cornwell-Clyne, Angela (*née* Brackenbury), 65
Coronet Romance Club, 183
Coward, Sir Noel, 122, 136
Creed, Charles, 169
Crystal Palace, 57, 59, 62

Daily Express, 169, 173
Daily Sketch, 136
Dark Corridor, 184–5
Davis, Brigadier Kits, 158
Dealtry, Adrian, 33, 34, 37

Dealtry, Cosmo, 33, 60, 80, 101
Dealtry, Herbert Arthur Berkeley
  (D. R.'s step-father), 21, 31–
  46, 50, 52, 54, 57, 60–3, 67–70,
  73, 75–9, 84, 101, 102
Dearden, Harold, 119
Dell, Ethel M., 33, 137
De Mille, Cecil B., 35
De Mille, Mrs., 35–6
Derville, Anthony, 177
Dowson, Ernest, 137
Dulverton, 119
Du Maurier, Sir Gerald, 119
Dundee, 71–3, 106
Dundee Courier, 73

Eaton Terrace, 145, 146
Eddy, Mary Baker, 29
Edinburgh, 147–51
Eels, Aubrey, 122
Ellis Island, 43
Ervine, St. John, 121
Evans, Elsie, 33–4, 100

Farouk, King of Egypt, 164
'Fidelis' convent, Upper Nor-
  wood, 53–60, 69
Five Ashes, Mayfield, Sussex, 28,
  32
Fleetway House Press, 104, 105
Fleming, Ian, 180
Flight into Fear (Gerard), 161
Flushing, N.Y., 27, 46–7
Forget-me-not Novels, 99, 104,
  105
Fox Hill, Norwood, 60, 62
Foyle, Christina, 169, 178–9, 183
Foyle, William, 179
Furnace Pond Cottage, Slaug-
  ham, 124–5, 178, 181
Further Outlook, 122–3

Garcia, Manuel, 15
Gartside, John, 168
Gartside, Leontine, 168
Gartside, Peter, 168, 174
Gartside, Phyllis, 168, 174
General Strike (1926), 110
Gerard, Francis, 161–3
Gerard, Mrs., 161–3
Gielgud, Val, 122
Girl's Weekly, 96
Golding, Louis, 169

Goodner, Carol, 122
Gray, Donald, 168
Griffith, Adrian, 112, 175–7
Griffith, Catherine, 176–7
Griffith, John, 112
Griffith, Maud, 112, 113, 176
Groom, Sydney, 63, 80, 83–4, 91,
  97, 101, 102, 130, 137, 154
Groves, William, 104, 105
Gynt, Greta, 168

Hackett, Walter, 120
Handy Stories, 106
Hanworth, Dorothy (*née* Robins),
  82, 90, 96, 98, 103
Hanworth, William, 90, 103
Hastings, Mary (Lady Hastings),
  113, 118
Hastings, Sir Patrick, 113–14,
  118, 119
Hathaway, Hélène, 29, 30, 65, 66
Haywards Heath, 114, 115, 181–2
Heat Wave, 119–22
Herbert, A. P. (Sir Alan), 179
Heritage, Kenneth, 160
Hervey, Marjorie, 125–6, 130
Hitler, Adolf, 144–6
Hobbs, Jack, 122, 123
Hodder and Stoughton, 110, 171
Hopkinson, Maurice and
  Barbara, 158
Horton, Admiral Sir Max, 157
House of the Seventh Cross, 182
Hulbert, Claude, 118
Hutchinson, Frances, 16, 50, 51,
  78
Hutchinson, Sir George, 16, 50,
  51, 78, 155
Hutchinson, Walter, 155

Ideas, 106
Interference, 119, 121
Irving, Sir Henry, 111
Irving, Laurence, 122
Ivanič, Milan, 184
Ivanič, Rosalind, *see* Sutton,
  Rosalind
Ivy Restaurant, 135–6

Jackson, Sir Hugh and Lady, 134

Keeble, Harold, 173
Khamsin, 165

Klein, Adrian, *see* Cornwell-Clyne, Adrian
Klein, Charles, 19, 25–6, 35–6, 46
Klein, Daryl (brother of D. R.), 18, 25, 26, 61–2
Klein, Herman (father of D. R.), 14–31, 50–2, 61, 65–8, 100; marriage, 15–17; career, 18, 21; elopement of wife, 21; leaves for America, 22; third marriage, 30
Klein, Ivy, 62
Klein, Kathleen Clarice Louise (*née* Cornwell) (mother of D. R.), 16–24, 28–57, 59–73, 76–80, 86–98, 101, 102, 130, 137–8, 154, 169; elopement, 21; second marriage, 28; writings, 44, 51–2, 84, 106; loss of second husband, 76–8; marriage to Sydney Groom, 83–4, 91; death, 171–2
Klein, Lilian, 25–9, 46
Klein, Philip, 25, 26
Klein, Sibyl, 17, 22, 24–6, 68–9
Komisarjevsky, Theodore, 122

Lawton, Frank, 119
Leigh, Vivien, 136
Lemon, Harriet, 178
Life and Love, 136
Lloyd-Jones, 'Buster', 173
Lodge, Ethel, 60
Lodge, Kenneth, 60
Lodge, Toby, 60–1
Los Angeles, 37
Love, Miss ('Nanna'), 19–20, 22, 24
Lyons, Ken, 151

McIndoe, Sir Archibald, 180–1
Mackay, Graham, 151
Mario (*maître d'hotel*), 135
Marshall, Herbert, 119–22
Maschwitz, Eric, 146
Matthews, Jessie, 183
Maugham, Somerset, 116–17
Melville, Alan, 183
Menuhin, Nola, 132–4
Menuhin, Yehudi, 133–4
Messel, Oliver, 145
Michelmore, Cliff, 178
Mills and Boon, 136

Montgomery–Campbell, Archie, 14
Moore, Jill Esmond, 118
Morley, Robert, 183
Morton, Digby, 135, 139, 152, 157, 169
Murder in Mayfair, 132
Murley, Annie, 160
Murley, Peter, 160
Musicians and Mummers (Herman Klein), 67

Neilson-Terry, Phyllis, 120, 121
New York, 25–30, 43–7
Newnes magazines, 105
Newquay, 62–3, 71, 73, 84
Nichols, Beverley, 183
Nicholson, Ivor, 136
Nightingale, Naomi (Lady Boynton), 59
Noble One, The, 171
Nordica, Madame, 23
Novello, Ivor, 124–5, 131–2, 135

Observer, The, 137
Ocean Beach, California, 38–9
Oliver, Dossie (*née* Hutchinson), 78
Oliver, Edward, 78
Oliver, Guy, 78
Olivier, Laurence (Lord Olivier), 118
Ouida, 112

Paderewski, Ignace, 19
Pam's Paper, 106
Panama Canal, 42, 44–8, 50
Panting, Phyllis (Phyllis Digby Morton), 135, 152, 155
Papadakis, George, 165
Pearson, 'Blossom', 160–1, 172
Pearson, Jack, 141, 150, 160
Pearson, Maria, 160
Pearson, O'Neill (Neill), 140–3, 146–61, 164, 166–8, 172, 173, 177, 179, 181, 183, 184; marriage to D. R., 147; in West Africa during war, 154, 158
Pearson, Pat, 141, 150
Pearson, Sarah, 160
Peg's Paper, 105
People, The, 106

Pertwee, John (Jon), 111, 119, 183, 185
Pertwee, Kitty, 175
Pertwee, Michael, 9–12, 111, 119, 183
Pertwee, Roland, 9, 14, 111–12, 117–22, 135, 175
Plomley, Roy, 184–5
P.N.E.U. School, Burgess Hill, 115
Ponders, Margaretting, 87–94, 103
Poppy's Paper, 105
Porth, 33–4, 101
Porth Bean, 70, 71, 73, 77, 78, 101
Powell, William, 122

Queen's Club Gardens, 51, 60
Quigley, Janet, 177

Rathbone, Basil, 122
Reid, Pat, 184
Rix, Brian, 119
Robins, Aimée, 87–9, 92–4, 103
Robins, Alice (*née* Sibthorpe), 82, 83, 87–8, 90
Robins, Anne (daughter of D. R.), 114, 115, 143, 146, 151, 155, 166–8, 184
Robins, Arthur Howis, 80–5, 92–100, 102–8, 110, 112–15, 117, 124, 134, 135, 137, 138, 143, 145–7; meets D. R., 80; early life, 81–2; family, 82–3, 85, 87–94; engagement to D. R., 85; marriage, 91; divorce, 146; death, 172
Robins, Denise: birth, 18–19; early memories, 19–21; in New York, 25–30, 43–7; with mother and step-father, 30–5; in California, 37–40; in convent school, 48–9; return to England, 50–1; at 'Fidelis' convent school, 53–60, 69; journalism in Dundee, 71–3, 106; and First World War, 75–86; love affairs, 74–6; and Arthur Robins, 80–5; engagement, 85; marriage, 91; short stories, 96; births of children, 97–8, 108, 114; novelettes and newspaper serials, 104–7; first novel, 110; amateur theatricals, 117–19; collaboration in plays, 119–23; and Neill Pearson, 140–3; divorce, 146; remarriage, 147; and Second World War, 147–58; serious illness, 159–60; hundredth novel, 168–9; death of mother and first husband, 171–2; TV & broadcasting, 177–8, 184–5
Robins, Enid, 88, 89, 93
Robins, Eve Louise (daughter of D. R.), 97–8, 100–2, 104, 107–9, 114, 123, 143–6, 151, 155–7, 159, 166
Robins, Harry, 82, 83, 87–94, 96, 102, 103, 108
Robins, Howis, 88–9
Robins, Patricia Denise (daughter of D. R.), 107–9, 114, 123, 143, 146, 151, 155, 159, 161–7, 169, 174, 178
Robins, Vaughan ('Goldie'), 82, 83, 88, 90, 102–4
Robinson, Alice, 16, 17, 21, 22, 50, 51, 73–5, 78
Robinson, Myrtle, 78
Romantic Novelists Association, 179–80, 183
Ross, Harry (Sir Henry), 150
Rosse, Countess of, 145
Ruck, Berta, 169

St. Anselm, Mother, 59
St. Benedict, Mother, 57
St. Columb Minor, 33, 100, 101
San Diego, 37–8
San Francisco earthquake, 38–40
Sanders, George, 122, 123
Sangster-Simmonds, Barnard, 76
Science and Health (Eddy), 29
Scott-Moncrieffe, Joanne, 177
Sealed lips, 110
Shaw, Bernard, 116
She, 170
Sherborne Castle, 158–9
Shiner, Ronald, 122
Shoreham-by-Sea, 73, 75, 76
Sloane Street, D. R.'s flat in, 135, 146
Spain, Nancy, 169, 170, 183
Strachey, Jack, 146

190

Strange Meeting, 169
Streatfeild, Noel, 118
Stuart, Alex, 179
Suez Canal Zone, 165
Sunday Dispatch, 136, 137
Sunday Times, 16
Sutton, Annabel, 166
Sutton, Charles Murray ('John'), 156–7, 159, 166
Sutton, Eve, *see* Robins, Eve
Sutton, Murray, 166
Sutton, Rosalind Eve, 159, 160, 174, 184
Swanson, Gloria, 135

Tallent, Helen, 151
Tallent, John, 151
Tangier, 126–30
Tate, Mary and Norman, 140
Tempest, Dame Marie, 135
Temple Chambers, 17
Thomson, D. C., 51, 70–2, 96
Thomson, Mrs., 70–2
Titanic, sinking of, 57
Todd, Ann, 120
Tomlinson, Sir Thomas, 160

Torremolinos, 125
Trevor, Captain Dudley, 161–2, 164
Triumph of the Rat, The, 132

Van Damm, Shirley, 170, 183
Victoria, Queen, 20

Watson, Bernard, 136
Weekend Novels, 105
Weekly Welcome, 51–2, 96
Wells, H. G., 135
Werner Laurie, Joan, 169–70
White, Harry ('Bill'), 79
White, Rosamund, 79
Whitehall Court, 18, 20, 111, 117
Whitlock, Louise, 98
Wilson, Catherine, *see* Griffith, Catherine
Winn, Godfrey, 169
Wiseman, Berty, 168, 169
Wiseman, Nancy, 168, 169
With the Chinks (Daryl Klein), 62
Woman and Beauty, 135, 155
Woman's Friend, 106
Woman's Hour, 177

DENISE ROBINS' ROMANTIC FICTION
AVAILABLE IN CORONET BOOKS

☐	19931 8	The Secret Hour	50p
☐	02896 3	Never Give All	60p
☐	21802 9	Never Look Back	60p
☐	18291 1	The Snow Must Return	60p
☐	15085 8	Brief Ecstasy	60p
☐	01459 8	The Noble One	60p
☐	17850 7	Desire Is Blind	60p
☐	12783 X	Infatuation	60p
☐	20809 0	Dark Corridor	60p
☐	12959 X	Strange Meeting	60p
☐	02259 0	To Love Again	60p
☐	18300 4	Do Not Go My Love	50p
☐	01065 7	I Should Have Known	50p
☐	20756 6	Twice Have I Loved	50p
☐	15097 1	You Have Chosen	60p

All these books are available at your local bookshop or newsagent, or can be ordered direct from the publisher. Just tick the titles you want and fill in the form below.

Prices and availability subject to change without notice.

....

CORONET BOOKS, P.O. Box 11, Falmouth, Cornwall.
Please send cheque or postal order, and allow the following for postage and packing:

U.K. – One book 19p plus 9p per copy for each additional book ordered, up to a maximum of 73p.

B.F.P.O. and EIRE – 19p for the first book plus 9p per copy for the next 6 books, thereafter 3p per book.

OTHER OVERSEAS CUSTOMERS – 20p for the first book and 10p per copy for each additional book.

Name ....

Address ....

....